# STUMPED

One cricket umpire,

two countries.

Richard Harrison

This book is dedicated to the memory of my friend and mentor John Allen.

# FOREWORD

Who in their right mind would want to be a cricket umpire?

Several years ago, when a friend of mine told me that he was umpiring cricket matches each weekend in a local league, I asked him with the most sincere disbelief; 'What on earth do you want to do that for?'

He gave me every assurance that he actually enjoyed spending his Saturdays 'in the middle,' and as close as we were, I found it very difficult to understand just how or why.

Cricket umpiring had always struck me as an entirely thankless task, and at times, a quite brutal endeavour.

Umpires were uniformed, yet invisible, and largely ignored, until such time as they were called upon to actually make a decision.

Once they did, they were on a hiding to nothing, almost certain to upset someone in the process of simply doing their best.

Happily there have always been those who are willing, and for the most part capable, of fulfilling an umpiring role in leagues and competitions all over the world, and it is fair to say that the game simply couldn't exist without them.

This book charts my own, entirely unplanned journey into cricket umpiring. It is intended to celebrate the most wonderful, complex and extraordinary game in the world, while paying tribute to the tremendous characters, colleagues and players that I have met along the way.

It is fair to say I am a total convert when it comes to cricket umpiring, and while there have been times when the role has been challenging, frustrating and even difficult; it has remained throughout both a joy and a privilege.

No game other than cricket has such a fascinating complexity, and such a long, rich and storied history.

Lest anyone be in any doubt, consider this;

Games have rules. Cricket has laws.

# CHAPTER ONE
# HOW'S THAT?!

Much of my youth was spent watching Dennis Lillee, as he charged in from the Southern Stand end of the MCG, in Test Matches against England and the West Indies.

The noise of the crowd would reach a fever pitch, as he delivered the ball, and ascend into a wild crescendo if it should crash into the batsman's pads, or (perhaps) collect a faint edge of willow, as it continued on its journey towards the wicket keeper.

Lillee himself would then execute a violent (yet balletic), mid air about face, landing in the middle of the pitch, his feet firmly planted on its surface, knees bent and arms outstretched, as he fashioned a crazed and desperate plea towards the umpire.

Rodney Marsh and the Chappell brothers would invariably join in. Their arms raised high in the air, conducting the crowd in a swelling unison of demand that would flood the entire stadium.

It was nothing if not great theatre and with the umpire himself now firmly in the spotlight, he need only raise one arm and a single finger to delight at least most of the audience, or shake his head from side to side, dismiss the appeal and be immediately cast as deaf, blind, an incompetent fool or all three.

Who wouldn't want that?

# CHAPTER TWO
## SEVENOAKS

I had been living in England for the best part of three years, and in Sevenoaks, Kent for about nine months.

Sevenoaks is a delightful and attractive medieval market town, that retains much of the character and architecture of centuries past. In fact, the estate agents that brokered the lease of my flat were located amid an original network of narrow, intersecting lanes that lay just off the High Street, appropriately called 'The Shambles.'

It was a fascinating place to visit, although I soon fell out of love with their dangerously low 16th century ceiling, having 'collected' it more times than I care to remember.

The Sevenoaks Vine cricket ground was located at the bottom end of the High Street, and needless to say home to the local club.

The land itself is believed to have once housed a

vineyard that was leased by the Archbishop of Canterbury, while seven Oak trees were planted at its northern edge in 1902, to mark the coronation of King Edward VII.

Six of those trees were destroyed in the 'Great Storm of 1987,' whereupon another seven were planted to replace them later that same year.

I am not entirely sure why seven trees were planted to replace six, and I dare say the arithmetic has confused many a visitor, as they strolled among the famous 'eight oaks,' while watching a game on the Vine.

The club was formed in 1734, and notable for the fact it was the first location in the country where cricket was played with three stumps instead of two, when Hambledon played England in a match on the Vine in 1777.

The addition of a third stump is largely attributed to one of the fastest, and most ferocious (albeit underarm), bowlers of the time. Edward 'Lumpy' Stevens was an estate worker at the nearby Knole Park, and someone who could deliver a cricket ball, that would often penetrate a batsman's defences, only for it to travel between two upright stumps, while failing to dislodge the single horizontal bail that sat above them.

I think Stevens deserves more notoriety and recognition than he currently enjoys. At the time, he may well have been a humble gardener, but how many people can lay claim to the fact they have made a significant and fundamental difference to how an international game is played?

The cricket ground was gifted to the town of Sevenoaks in 1773 by the 3rd Duke of Dorset, a man who can realistically boast being one of the very first supporters of women's cricket.

In 1777 the Duke convinced his mistress (the Countess of Derby), to arrange and host a ladies' cricket match, having earlier published a letter in a society magazine of the day, encouraging 'Ladies of quality and fashion to take up cricket.'

Fortunately, it is an invitation that many continue to accept to this day.

My flat was located on St. John's Hill, which was itself an extension of the High Street, and little more than a stone's throw from the Vine itself.

Weekend cricket matches certainly completed the town's aesthetic during the summer months, but winters were a different proposition altogether. It was often bitterly cold, and losing daylight around four o'clock certainly took some getting used to.

Throughout the colder months in particular, I was always grateful for the fact that a pile of local newspapers was delivered to the foyer of my building each Thursday afternoon, as (if nothing else), they gave me access to the week's television listings.

I never really paid much attention to the local news, but one day I did take note of the fact a famous Lime tree, which had been standing in the outfield of the Kent County Cricket Ground at Canterbury, had been uprooted and destroyed in a gale.

It was the lead story on the back page and as a consequence, the first article I was likely to read.

The twenty seven metre tall tree pre-dated the establishment of the ground itself in 1847, and it was believed to have already been some forty years old at that time.

The tree had long been the subject of some specific local playing conditions, given it was growing several metres inside the designated boundary.

Its demise was certainly a shame, but happily the club intended carrying on the tradition, and planting another in its place.

More to the point however, there was a separate paragraph added to the article, alerting readers to the fact, that a local cricket association was presenting a series of training courses for aspiring umpires, over the course of the winter. Venues included Maidstone, Tunbridge Wells and Sevenoaks, while anyone interested, should contact a fellow called Ian Fraser on the phone number listed.

As much as I loved the game, I hadn't played for the best part of twenty years, and I had never umpired a match in my life. All the same, I thought that enrolling in the course, might give me a chance to address my burgeoning television addiction, and escape the flat once a week.

I made the call and after a brief chat with Ian, I was on board.

# CHAPTER THREE
## TRAINING

The training course was co-ordinated by a handful of members of the Sevenoaks Cricket Umpires and Scorers' Association, and presented each week on a Wednesday evening, at the local rugby club.

The club itself was a twenty minute walk from my flat, and the route took me (rather appropriately), directly across the Sevenoaks Vine cricket ground. Though often covered in snow, it still seemed appropriate to include on my weekly itinerary.

I turned up on the first night, and parted with £30 in exchange for a text book, a copy of the MCC Laws of Cricket, and a bound copy of the course notes.

The presenters (all veterans of the craft), were dressed as cricket umpires, as they spoke to a dozen or so of us, with the aid of a screen, a projector, and a Power Point presentation.

The course was presented over ten weeks, covering

all forty two of the game's historic and at times complex laws. Those who would see it through to the end, would have the opportunity to sit an entry level exam, and (all being well), secure an official umpiring qualification.

The atmosphere was warm (even if the room wasn't), and friendly. I was the only Australian, which granted me novelty status almost immediately, and I felt quite certain I would enjoy myself. And that was despite the fact we were expected to complete a weekly homework assignment.

Each evening's presentation was very thorough and detailed, usually lasting at least two hours, while our homework was complicated, and marked very harshly, with no shortage of red ink. As a consequence, class numbers gradually dwindled, to about four or five after ten weeks.

Having stuck it out for the duration, I thought I should at least sit the exam, as if nothing else, I wanted to have something to show for all of the time and effort I had devoted.

One of the presenters explained to what remained of the class, that the exam would be held at the HSBC cricket ground in Beckenham - a town on the south-eastern outskirts of London.

Recognising me as 'from out of town,' he addressed me specifically.

'Richard. Do you know where the HSBC ground is in Beckenham?'

I replied; 'I don't even know where Beckenham is,' which generated a ripple of laughter, before I was presented with a very detailed set of directions, that would in fact lead me straight to the ground, assuming I could catch a train to the local station.

On the day in question, I caught the train, made my way to the ground, and arrived in plenty of time. I registered, and was ushered upstairs into a room which housed fifty or so small desks, arranged in rows facing a large screen, ahead of a projector that was suspended from the ceiling.

The exam was structured in a multiple choice format, with a presenter reading a series of sixty questions aloud and in turn.

Each question was also displayed on the screen, while those present were tasked with marking the correct answer on the sheets provided.

I sat in the front row, as the room started to fill, recognising a couple of my Sevenoaks contemporaries, among an eclectic gathering, that must have completed the same training course in other parts of the county.

The questions followed a logical match day sequence, testing our knowledge of the procedures and processes that umpires should undertake while inspecting the ground, before speaking with the captains and executing the toss.

Thereafter, we moved on to various 'No ball' scenarios, all of which garnered additional concentration, as a single incorrect answer in this sequence alone would result in a fail.

The exam took ninety minutes to complete, while our results would be confirmed by mail, in a week or two.

80% was considered a pass, and I was feeling quietly confident when I was greeted by one of the Sevenoaks contingent, just as I was leaving. I hadn't actually spoken to him before, as he had only attended some of the classes, but he offered to give me a lift home, which I gratefully accepted.

He too was very confident, as he had been playing the game for several years - most recently for the Sevenoaks 2nd XI. As we drove along, he asked me what answer I had given to any number of questions, whereupon it soon became apparent (to me anyway), that one of us had almost certainly failed. I was pretty sure that it wasn't me, and rather than embarrass my 'driver,' I became rather vague in my recollections and simply responded 'So did I,' when he confirmed each answer that he had submitted.

It was quite a long trip, as I tried to steer the conversation in a different direction, at least until we passed a landmark I could recognise, in the event I would have to walk the rest of the way.

Finally, we reached the outskirts of Sevenoaks, and before long I was alighting outside my flat. I thanked my colleague and wished him all the best, in the fervent hope that he did not intend pursuing cricket umpiring as a career.

A week or so later, my results hadn't yet arrived, when head tutor John Allen rang to congratulate me. Apparently I had missed a perfect score by just one mark.

For what it's worth, umpires (while ultimately responsible for the correctness of the score), are not in fact obliged to confirm it during a drinks break.

# CHAPTER FOUR
## MY DEBUT

John Allen was a delightful man. Calm, friendly and possessed of a very gentle, self deprecating sense of humour, he seemed to have all of the qualities a cricket umpire would need, and it came as no surprise to learn that he was indeed very well liked and highly respected in the field.

John also managed a panel of umpires that he appointed to various village and school games in and around Kent. I fairly jumped at the chance to join, and before long my very first umpiring assignment was confirmed.

I was told that I would be standing with an experienced colleague in a pre-season practice match on a Sunday at Meopham - a community that boasts the curious title of 'The Longest Village in Britain.'

I invested in the necessary attire – a broad brimmed white hat, white coat, black trousers and white trainers. In addition to bowler's markers, a set of bails, bowling cards, a note pad, a couple of clutch pencils (as I didn't trust using a biro in the rain), scissors, band aids and a pocket sized, laminated 'cheat sheet,' that listed some unlikely scenarios and associated penalties, should a veritable 'blue mooner' present itself.

Meopham had arranged to play a neighbouring team from New Ifield on the village green.

The Green itself was located alongside the A227 and appropriately enough, opposite a pub called The Cricketers' Arms.

I was warmly welcomed into the club's delightful and quaint pavilion, to see various photographs of the Melbourne Cricket Ground adorning the walls.

Apparently, a touring group of Australian MCC members continue to play a fixture at Meopham during each Ashes tour. I dare say it was something John was well aware of, and I don't think he could have found a more appropriate venue for me to make my umpiring debut.

I changed in the umpires' room at the base of the stairs, before introducing myself to my colleague and the two captains. New Ifield won the toss, chose to bat and we took the field under a clear blue sky.

I chose to stand at the pavilion end and having meticulously inspected the stumps, crease markings and counted the fielders, I tossed the ball to the opening bowler. I confirmed the batsman's guard, checked my watch, indicated the bowler's mode of delivery, then took up a position and prepared to launch my umpiring career with the call of 'Play!'

I concentrated heavily, as the bowler approached and the batsman faced up. As the bowler entered his delivery stride, I carefully focussed on the position of his feet (in the event that he might deliver a No ball), being sure to move my eyes only and not my head, as we had been taught. The idea being that I could more readily detect just where the ball might have pitched, in the event of an appeal for leg before wicket.

I held my breath and fixed my gaze, as the bowler released the ball.

Moments later, the batsman let a harmless and perfectly innocuous delivery, travel outside of his off stump, and through to the wicket keeper.

It was, by any measure, spectacularly uneventful.

As the game progressed, I was still feeling quite nervous but enjoying myself immensely, and after successfully negotiating the first few overs, I was presented with my very first 'challenge.'

I was standing at the striker's end (square leg), when the New Ifield captain launched a powerful pull shot, heaving the ball high in the air and directly over my head. I turned around, following the flight of the ball, watching it disappear over the boundary, when I caught sight of a dark green, late model Jaguar, travelling south along the A227.

Even my rudimentary grasp of physics had indicated that the descent of the ball, and path of the vehicle, were almost certain to coincide and sure enough they did with an almighty thud.

My colleague dutifully signalled 'six,' as with a screech of brakes, the Jag quickly ground to a halt. The driver got out, inspected the damage, and with an angry, determined gait, marched straight onto the field, making a bee line for me.

I quickly recounted all of the 42 Laws I had studied, together with the field craft and personnel management solutions we had been taught, but I couldn't recall anything that came under the heading 'Irate motorist invades field of play.'

The driver began protesting the damage to his car, just as one of the Meopham players ran over, suggesting he speak to their president, who could explain the process involved in making a claim on the club's insurance. Apparently damage to moving cars was covered, but woe betide anyone foolish, or brave enough to park alongside what is quite a small ground.

The driver marched off to the pavilion, where I dare say his issue was addressed with both courtesy and concern, as he emerged a few minutes later, and made his way back to his car, possessed of a relatively calm and relaxed demeanour.

The New Ifield innings continued without any further serious incident, before we adjourned for tea mid afternoon.

The English cricket tea is a source of great pride amongst villages and clubs all over the country, and rarely is any trouble or expense spared in its preparation or presentation. This day, Meopham put on a spread that included sandwiches, cakes, muffins, crisps, soft drinks, tea and coffee. I reckon I have attended weddings in Australia that weren't as generously catered. I just wish they had bigger plates, as that might have saved me the trouble of piling on a third helping.

The designated thirty minutes flew by, and we soon took the field again. Me with a poppy seed muffin stuffed in my trouser pocket.

The second innings passed without any great drama, and the match concluded with everyone shaking hands, before we retired to the bar in the pavilion.

It was well and truly dark by the time I left, having enjoyed a good few pints of the local beer, and I was only too happy to accept a lift home, before returning the next day to collect my car.

It was terrific getting to know some of the players and club officials and the MCC connection made it a really special occasion.

Village greens and cricket grounds lie at the heart of towns and hamlets all over the country, and for me it was both a delight and a privilege to umpire my first cricket match in England. I felt that I had a made a small contribution, in the birth place of a game with such a wonderful history and a rich tradition.

# CHAPTER FIVE
# TONBRIDGE FESTIVAL

My next umpiring appointment was in fact to a series of games played at Tonbridge School - one of the most expensive and privileged educational institutions in the country.

Each year's 'Cricket Festival' saw Tonbridge play host to teams representing schools from Australia, South Africa and England.

This particular year the roster included St. Peter's Adelaide, Chester House from Cape Town and the Millfield School from Somerset.

Each school would play the other once, on each of three consecutive days, with two games staged simultaneously. One would be played on the school's main ground - 'The Head' and another on an adjoining ground known as 'Martin's.'

It was hard to imagine a more perfect setting for a game of cricket, and I was thrilled to be appointed to

'The Head' on the first day.

Tonbridge played host to Chester House, and I was rostered to stand with Joe Townsend, the 'Homework Tsar' from the training course, and an umpire with some thirty years of experience, which included any number of County 2nd XI championship matches. No pressure then.

'The Head' was located at the very heart of the school grounds and opposite a limestone chapel, that in any other setting could probably pass for a cathedral.

An impressive scoreboard and elevated scorers' box was housed next to the pavilion, while an assortment of cars, parents and spectators were dotted around the boundary.

The pitch was immaculate, and the outfield lush and green, as soon after the toss, the two teams followed Joe and me onto the field.

I took up a position at the northern end, securing the honour of the day's first over, and I was busily taking in the magnificent surrounds, when I heard a voice call out in the distance.

'Sir!'

I thought one of the boys was addressing a teacher, as nothing resonated with me.

'Sir!' the voice repeated, a little louder this time, as my

eyes scanned the chapel and its neighbouring buildings.

'Excuse me. Umpire!' the bowler shouted.

I turned around sharply.

'Oh. I'm sorry' I said. 'Are you talking to me?'

Needless to say, I granted his request for a practice run through. After all, manners should count for something.

The first innings saw Tonbridge accumulate a healthy score of 234 runs from their allocated 45 overs, before we adjourned to the pavilion for a roast lunch. It was the boys' responsibility to serve their teachers, and the umpires and I made a point of consuming just the one glass of wine, lest there be any suggestion of influence or distraction during the afternoon session.

Forty minutes later, we returned for the second innings, whereupon some of the Tonbridge boys seemed to enjoy the nick names I had invented for them, and written on my bowling card. 'Curly' and 'Lefty' certainly did. As for 'Smart Arse,' I am not so sure.

I was lucky enough to be appointed to 'The Head' for the second day and on the third I was allocated to the game on 'Martin's.'

The match may have been scheduled on the school's second ground, but if I ever umpire a game as exciting and enjoyable again, I will count myself very lucky.

Chester House from Cape Town was sent in by St. Peter's Adelaide, making 227 runs before we enjoyed another sumptuous lunch.

St. Peter's made steady progress in their run chase but lost wickets at regular intervals, which kept the result of the game very much in the balance throughout.

Word had spread that a close finish was likely to ensue and after the match on 'The Head' finished early, a large crowd of players, parents and students surrounded 'Martin's.'

The match came down to the last over. St. Peter's needed 10 runs to win but with nine wickets down, just one mistake would end the day for the South Australians.

I was standing at the striker's end, when the Chester House captain entrusted the crucial last over to his talented leg spinner - a fellow who had claimed a number of scalps earlier in the day.

The St. Peter's batsman took a brave and aggressive approach, trying to hit the first ball of the over into a neighbouring post code.

He missed, and the ball landed safely in the wicket keeper's gloves.

The next delivery was called and signalled 'wide,' before the following one was clipped through the leg side for two.

Four balls remaining. Seven runs to win.

Another 'wide' served only to increase the tension, before the next delivery yielded a single.

Three balls left and five runs to win.

Another ambitious swing, and another miss followed, before a repeat dose from the next delivery secured a thick edge past the keeper, over the slips and across the boundary for four.

The scores were tied, with one delivery remaining.

I can remember thinking what a fabulous three days it had been, what a tremendous game I was witnessing, and that conversations on the long flights home for both teams the next day, would surely be liberally punctuated with the outcome of this game in particular.

St. Peter's needed just a single to win, and I was surprised to see the striker advance down the pitch, just as the bowler tossed the ball in the air. One run would win the day. Hitting a six was just showing off.

The striker planted his left foot in the middle of the pitch, and hurled his bat at the ball, completing a wide arc, as his arms came full circle, all but throwing himself off balance in the process.

Suffice to say he missed, and stranded a good three metres out of his crease, could only watch as the ball travelled towards the stumps.

As it happened, the wicket keeper (in his haste to take hold of the ball and stump the striker), managed to dislodge the bails with his gloves, a split second before the ball itself hit the stumps.

Strictly speaking that is a 'No ball,' and I (as the striker's end umpire), was obliged under the laws of the game, to call and signal just that, effectively awarding a one run penalty to the batting side. The ball itself would be considered 'Dead' upon the call, the batsman rendered 'Not out,' and as a consequence St. Peter's would win the day.

I did no such thing.

I clearly saw the wicket keeper knock the bails off, as the striker himself was stranded way out of his ground. The ball ultimately hit the stumps and but for the keeper's indiscretion, the batsman would have most certainly been bowled.

I had no desire to ruin what was (to my mind), a very fair and memorable outcome to a great game, and I simply pretended that I didn't see what happened.

Happily no one else seemed to notice. All the players

shook hands, and the overall mood among them and several hundred spectators was warm and friendly.

At least, it was until the Chester House coach came onto the field. He marched towards the umpires, and began berating my colleague for calling two wides in the last over, when (apparently), he hadn't 'called one all day!'

His manner was very aggressive, and he seemed almost out of control, when I stepped in to defend my colleague.

'Now hang on a minute mate' I said, as I prepared to confess the crime that would have otherwise gifted the Adelaide boys a win.

He turned towards me and faced me with a wild, startled glare. It looked to me as if his eyes were likely to fall out of their sockets any moment.

'You' he said excitedly, pointing his finger in my face. 'You!'

I pinned my shoulders back, as I summoned an appropriate response, should he say anything more.

'You' he continued, 'are the best umpire we've had on our whole trip!'

He took hold of my hand, shook it furiously, said 'Thank you' and walked away.

That evening I gave John Allen a call.

During the training course, John and his colleagues had often referred to 'Law 43' - an apocryphal law of common sense that cricket umpires should seek to apply wherever possible, in delicate and difficult situations.

I proudly told John, that I had in fact that very day invented 'Law 44.'

'Law 44?' he asked. 'What on earth is that?'

'Law 44' I repeated. 'If he sees fit, the umpire can do what he bloody well likes.'

# Chapter Six
## My First Season

John Allen and I had kept in regular contact, as he continued to present me with any number of weekend umpiring opportunities, for the months ahead.

I gratefully accepted each one, and discovered (once I had typed up the list and stuck it on the fridge), that I had in fact committed to umpiring every Saturday and Sunday for the entire the season.

My appointments were to various village, social, and school fixtures at clubs and grounds located in Kent and Sussex. Saturday games were competitive matches, while Sundays were generally reserved for friendlies.

The context of the games made little difference to me, as I was simply delighted to be there at all, while I managed to discover any number of hidden gems, amongst the towns and villages of England's south east.

I became a regular fixture, with a touring team known as 'The Chessmen,' who were for the most part, in the twilight of their playing careers.

The Chessmen toured around the south east playing Sunday friendlies and we became well acquainted, as a consequence of the obligatory post match pint, as much as anything that transpired on the field.

Chessmen matches were invariably played in a scrupulously fair manner. My umpiring role was often reduced to simply counting the balls in the over, as batsmen would invariably walk when caught behind, or trapped plumb LBW.

I can remember one Chess Batsman playing at a ball that a moment later landed safely in the wicket keeper's gloves. Without so much as a murmur from the bowler, or fielding side, he tucked his bat under his arm and marched off the field. I thought he must have a train to catch, but it later transpired that the ball had in fact, just barely brushed his glove.

Each game that I umpired seemed to be played in a setting that was even more delightful and picturesque than the last.

Cricket grounds were often bordered by trees that were centuries old, and in one instance a gentle stream ran along the length of the boundary.

Shipbourne Cricket Club leased the superbly named 'Fatting Pen Field' from the Fairlawne Estate - a fair patch of dirt, once owned by a family of National Hunt racehorse trainers that numbered the Queen Mother among their clients.

The club was sponsored by a pub in the nearby village, appropriately called 'The Chaser Inn,' where players and umpires would invariably convene after each game.

Shipbourne became a regular fixture (both home and away), and I soon became great friends with the club's players and officials.

Many were old boys of Tonbridge School, commuting from London each weekend to play.

'Fatting Pen Field' itself, was set back about a mile from the road, beyond an obscure entrance, that many a visiting team took some time to locate. Games often failed to start on time, after any number of players arrived late. An anomaly, that wasn't helped by the fact the 'locals' would often refuse any knowledge of just where the cricket club was located, if those asking failed to pronounce the name of the village correctly.

In addition to my weekend endeavours, I often stood in a Friday night fixture with the 'Old Oaks.' All of whom were ageing and former players of Sevenoaks Vine.

The Vine cricket ground was a five minute walk from my flat, my match fee was free beer and I had the opportunity to stand with Ian 'Fingers' Fraser, who first introduced me to the training course, a year or so before.

'Old Oaks' games were played at a fairly gentle pace, and on one occasion they inducted a young Australian into their ranks, before he joined the senior team on Saturdays.

He was a nineteen year old leg spinner/batsman from New South Wales, who had been living and playing 'up north,' before relocating to the south east, for the remainder of the season.

Quiet and softly spoken, he came on to bowl at my end, and I remember how I could hear the ball literally fizz out of his hand, such were the revolutions he managed to impart on it.

When he came in to bat, he confidently advanced down the pitch to the very first ball he faced, clipping it through mid wicket with precise timing.

I emailed a friend who lived in London the next day, suggesting he remember this kid's name, as I felt sure he was destined to play for Australia.

His name was Steven Smith.

The following day, I returned to the village ranks,

when I was appointed to stand in a game at Shoreham - a small village just north of Sevenoaks.

Luckily, not too far north, as I chose to walk home, after consuming several pints of the 'Dartford Wobbler' – a guest beer from a local micro brewery, that was on tap at the King's Head, where we gathered from late afternoon, after the game was washed out.

The pub itself was built in 1570, and I wasn't able stand upright in the bar, such was the height of the ceiling. I stayed perched on a stool until the pub closed, and it was time to stagger home.

Rain had interrupted play a couple of times earlier in the day, whereupon we decided to take an early tea.

I didn't particularly take to the spread of multi grain, cucumber, cheese and pickle sandwiches that were presented, and instead began piling a number of white bread and jam concoctions onto my plate, when I felt a tap on my shoulder.

'Excuse me,' a very gentle and kind looking woman said, 'but those are actually for the children.'

I looked down at the forlorn and disappointed face that belonged to a girl who looked about six. She was holding a small empty plate in front of her chest, as were another four or five of her contemporaries, who had very politely queued behind her. It must have looked like a scene from Oliver Twist.

I have rarely felt so ashamed.

My association with Ian Fraser and the Old Oaks, was to pay a healthy dividend later that season, when I was invited to umpire a couple of mid week matches on the Vine.

The Sevenoaks Cricket Club had arranged to stage a charitable event with 'Lashings,' a touring group of former international cricketers, who played against various club teams, as a means of generating funds for charity.

Ian and I would umpire free of charge, while the club would sell tickets to the matches, and tables for lunch, where guests would be seated with players and entertained by Zimbabwean international Henry Olanga's singing.

The Lashings player roster included the likes of Gordon Greenidge, Saqlain Mushtaq, Devon Malcolm and Wasim Jaffer, with Australia represented by Stuart Law.

The weather was kind, and the event drew a large crowd that gathered around the boundary for matches either side of lunch, against members of the Sevenoaks 1st and 2nd XIs.

It was quite a thrill to umpire a game with players whose autographs I had sought as child, even if their pace and veracity had dulled somewhat.

# CHAPTER SEVEN
## VILLAGE CRICKET

Village cricket is certainly alive and well in Kent.

So much so, that the county has two entirely separate village cricket competitions.

The Kent Village Cricket League and the Kent County Village League.

The Kent Village Cricket League has six divisions, each with twelve teams, for 72 in total.

The Kent County Village League, has seven divisions. The first six have ten teams, and the seventh has twelve for 72 in total.

Together the two competitions demonstrate all the trappings of an arms race, and anyone who wants to suggest that both leagues evolved to have exactly the same number of teams, at exactly the same time, entirely by coincidence, will get an argument from me.

For the most part, I was appointed to matches in

the Kent County Village League. Some were quite close by, such as Otford and Eynsford, while others were further afield such as Sissinghurst and Headcorn.

Travelling to and from games each weekend allowed me to discover some delightful towns and villages en route, and some wonderful cricket grounds once I had arrived.

Each club and each ground had its own history and tradition, while all had their own unique characteristics and eccentricities.

Some pavilions, and score boxes for that matter, featured thatched roofs, while the pavilion at Leigh, was located across a road from the ground itself.

Penshurst Park is a village club that was formed in 1752. It played its home games on a cricket ground that constituted the back yard of Penshurst Place, arguably the most glorious and magnificent 14th century mansion in the entire country.

The 'house' itself, cast an imposing figure over the entire ground, as it sat on the very edge of the boundary and it was hard not to feel intimidated by its presence and grandeur.

No batsman ever managed to smash a window while I was there, but I fear the owners might have set the dogs on anyone who did.

Over the course of the season, I was lucky enough to umpire several games at Meopham and Shipbourne in particular.

My sensible and conservative strategy, to always park some distance from the ground at Meopham, was vindicated one day, when a rather lusty straight drive made short work of a parked car's front passenger side window.

I suspect the owner may have been visiting some friends who resided in one of the many houses that bordered the ground, as there was no reaction amongst the playing group, officials or spectators at the time.

I recalled from my very first game, that any damage inflicted to cars driving alongside the ground was covered by the club's insurance, but not to those whose owners were foolish, or optimistic enough to park within the line of fire as it were.

I never saw the owner return and while he or she would face the prospect and expense of replacing a car window, at least they would be compensated by the fact a relatively new cricket ball was sitting on the driver's seat.

Much of the season was great fun and relatively uneventful, while I was often grateful for the fact I was standing with an experienced colleague.

I did have a bad day at Fordcombe however.

In the very first over of the match, I called 'No ball' for a front foot bowling violation, whereupon the bowler in question immediately disputed the decision, pointing at the marks in the pitch where he reckoned his foot had landed, arguing that his heel could not possibly have landed in front of the batting crease.

In the past, I had always managed to address the occasional dispute or argument quite calmly and politely, but for whatever reason, this day I decided to adopt an entirely inflexible and almost dictatorial approach.

I would not entertain any argument under any circumstances, and I made it abundantly clear to the bowler and his captain just who was in charge.

At this stage, the genie was well and truly out of the bottle, and I felt I had little choice other than to maintain a very strict, inflexible and unfriendly approach for the rest of the game.

It was not my finest hour and no doubt awkward and embarrassing for my colleague into the bargain.

Suffice it to say, it was a long day, as I struggled to maintain my focus and concentration throughout, while trying to justify the attitude and behaviour I had adopted, to myself as much as anyone.

I was very grateful when the match ended and I hit the road soon after, not staying for a pint in the local pub for the first time.

After mulling the experience over at home for a couple of hours, I picked up the phone and called John Allen. I told him exactly what had happened and he was, as ever, very kind and supportive.

He asked me if I wanted to report the player in question and I said 'No.'

'Was he abusive?' John asked.

'No, but I was' I said, adding 'Perhaps you should report me?'

At the end of the season, I was delighted to be invited to the Kent County Village League Presentation Dinner, by members of the Meopham Cricket Club, explaining to my friends at Shipbourne (who seemed mildly put out on the night), that the Meopham boys had in fact asked me first.

It was a great night and at one point, my 'legend status' was confirmed by one guest, as apparently I was the first umpire to ever stand up to one notoriously grumpy and aggressive individual at some point during the season.

Not at Fordcombe I hasten to add.

The Meopham boys were terrific company, and I

spent no small amount of time at the Shipbourne table as well, before we were entertained by an after dinner speech, from former English Test off spinner and latter day national selector, Geoff Miller.

I remembered Miller as the villain who took the slips catch, that Chris Tavare deflected from Ian Botham's bowling, after Allan Border and Jeff Thomson fell just 4 runs short, when needing to put on 74 for the last wicket, to win the 1982 Boxing Day Test. The Australians needed just 37 more runs at stumps on the fourth day, before I, together with a friend and a few hundred other optimists, made my way to the MCG the next morning, in the hope we might witness a miracle.

I was hoping that he wouldn't lead with that and to be fair he didn't. Instead, he delivered a very funny speech that included one anecdote where he was abused over the fence, by an angry home spectator in a Test Match at Headingley.

Having dismissed the West Indian (and arguably world's best) batsman Viv Richards quite early in the first session of the second day, he made his way towards the boundary, at the end of his over, to take up a designated fielding position.

Anticipating a generous round of applause once he

reached the fence, all he could hear was a solitary voice, calling out in a distinctive Yorkshire accent.

'You tosser Miller!' the spectator bellowed. 'I have just paid fifty quid to watch Richards bat!'

Sometimes you just can't win.

# CHAPTER EIGHT
# THE ORAL

My first season of umpiring had been a tremendous success. I had enjoyed myself immensely, made any number of new friends, and drunk quite a lot of beer.

My second season, brought with it an opportunity to advance, when I was invited to umpire in the Kent League and also to play again.

Kent League games would be played on Saturdays, which left Sundays free to play village friendlies with Shipbourne.

It seemed like the perfect balance, and save for the fact a few old muscles would have to come out of hibernation, I couldn't wait to get started.

Umpiring in the Kent League was a more professional endeavour, which meant attending meetings throughout the season and the prospect of sitting an oral exam.

I had breezed through my earlier multiple choice

exams, and arrived for my 'oral,' in a small room next to the kitchen, in the Wateringbury church hall.

Two examiners sat behind a table, while I perched on a chair in front of them.

'Now you are in for a bit of a grilling' one of them said.

He wasn't kidding.

Two hours later, having visualised and demonstrated countless match day scenarios, I found myself in the kitchen, nursing a thumping headache, as the examiners tallied my score.

Should I fail, I vowed never to return.

The tone was set early, when I was asked to explain what procedures and processes I should enact, when first arriving at the ground, and walking onto the field of play.

'What have you got with you?' one of the examiners asked.

I reeled off a list that included a counter, bowler's marker, a spare bail, pen, pair of scissors, sprig spanner, a couple of band aids and a bowling card.

'You've forgotten something' he said.

I added 'a positive mental attitude and cheerful disposition,' but he wasn't buying it.

'No. You've forgotten something' he said sternly.

'Beats me' I said.

'The ball!' he replied.

I fired back, 'My colleague's got it,' pointing to an imaginary associate to my left.

I thought it was pretty funny.

They didn't.

I had of course already factored in a mandatory deduction for being an Australian, but I managed to pass comfortably enough all the same.

# CHAPTER NINE
# THE PLAYING CAPER

The prospect of playing again wasn't quite as daunting, but it did represent a challenge all the same.

I had already acquired a Shipbourne club shirt, sweater and cap, but as the new season approached my shopping list was still quite long.

As luck would have it, the Bat and Ball sports shop in Sevenoaks was only a short walk from my flat, and I wandered down there one day to wave a few bats around.

Most of the major brands were all displayed, as was a name I wasn't the least bit familiar with.

Salix was a small Kent based outfit, owned and operated by a fellow called Andrew Kember, who had apparently served an apprenticeship with legendary Sussex bat maker John Newbery.

I could recognise a Salix cricket bat if I picked it up blind folded. I am not entirely sure why but they just felt different. They had a natural balance, and were very comfortable to hold - while adopting a makeshift batting stance, and executing a couple of phantom cover drives in a shop anyway. It was as if each one belonged in my hands, and the next Saturday morning I visited the factory.

I could have picked a better day and time. It was the eve of the cricket season, and the showroom was awash with fathers treating their sons, and established clients either upgrading, or dropping off bats to be repaired.

All the same, I was lucky enough to be introduced to Andrew, with whom I managed to strike an instant rapport.

I told him that picking up one of his bats, was like being upgraded to Business Class, and how much I admired the passion and craftsmanship that must be involved in creating each one.

I explained that I was in the market for a bat myself, whereupon he escorted me into the factory, and stood me in front of a shelved wall, full of crudely shaped 'clefts' of willow, with bat handles already inserted.

He took each one out in turn, retaining a handful that he inspected more closely. Once he had narrowed the stock down to three or four, he started hitting each one with a wooden mallet, asking me to do the same, and together we settled on one in particular, where the mallet fairly bounced off the face of the blade.

Over the course of the next hour or so, he shaped, sanded, and caressed a crude piece of willow into a bespoke masterpiece. He even filed, and shaped the base of the handle to suit my own grip, asking me to feel the weight and balance at every stage.

His concentration was immense and he seemed to be in some sort of hypnotic trance throughout, such was his focus and attention.

When the time came to pay, I added a kit bag, together with some pads and gloves, before a member of his staff assured me; 'No one gets a bat made for them like that,' and that mine was an indeed something special.

My new bat and I would debut in one of Shipbourne's Sunday friendlies, a week before the start of the Kent League season.

We were playing away at Speldhurst, and having lost the toss, were asked to bowl first.

Our captain was kind enough to let me field in the slips. Not that I was ever likely catch anything, but it did give me the opportunity to be closely involved in the game.

The match itself was very relaxed and friendly, while I noticed that a lot of the Speldhurst players were using bats that were branded 'Willo Stix,' with stickers of snakes and lizards plastered on the back of their blades.

When yet another batsman came to the crease, with a colourful Anaconda plastered on his, I chirped 'Gee you must be getting a pretty deal on those bats.'

I expected to be ignored, or at the very least treated to a stubborn, pithy reply, the likes of; 'Well they're good enough to smash you around with you dickhead.'

Instead he stepped towards me, showed me the label on the face of his blade, and said 'Yes, well they're made by a local company and we like to support them.'

It was a quite brilliant riposte, as I don't think I said another word for the rest of the innings.

Speldhurst put their 'Stix' to good use throughout the afternoon, amassing 183 runs before it was time for tea.

I was slotted to bat at number five, and indulged in a few sandwiches and cakes, secure in the knowledge I wouldn't be required immediately after the break.

Our third wicket fell with the score on 73, and I strode to the crease to join Ben Spokes, who was by this stage well set and half my age.

I managed to survive my first few deliveries, before deflecting a ball behind square leg, and setting off for my first run.

I shuffled towards the pavilion end, where my team mates had gathered, and as Ben and I passed each other mid pitch, he glanced across and said 'Come on. Three.'

I hadn't reached the other end before I peered back over my shoulder, calling out 'Three?! What are you fucking kidding?!' as a burst of laughter erupted from the boundary.

Suffice to say we completed a comfortable two, which, all things considered, I found quite sufficient.

Once the running arrangements had been sorted out, we managed to compile a healthy partnership, before Ben departed, with Shipbourne needing just two runs to win.

Andy Gillam then came to the crease and simply refused to score. In fact, at one point he stepped way across the pitch, allowing a ball that would otherwise have been called 'wide' to hit his leg.

At the end of the over, I asked what on earth he

was doing. He explained that I was on 49 and that if he or sundries should score the winning runs, it would deny me the opportunity to make a 50 on debut.

I thought he was being very generous, and told him so, when he confessed that his primary motivation was the fact that I would be expected to buy at least two jugs of beer after the game, if I did.

It would have been downright churlish to get out at that point, and fortunately I managed to get us home in the next over.

The beer I was expected to buy was Harvey's Sussex Bitter. In fact, it was always Harvey's Sussex Bitter, given our fixture secretary only scheduled games with clubs, who frequented pubs that had it on tap.

# CHAPTER TEN
## VILLAGE FRIENDLIES

Accepting an invitation to play cricket with Shipbourne each Sunday, was just about the best decision I have ever made.

The Sunday village friendly, is a quintessential element in the very fabric of the game in England, with any number of matches played each week all over the country.

All the same, I find it hard to believe there could be a more beautiful collection of cricket grounds, than those we played at throughout Kent and Sussex.

Venues like Withyham and Penshurst were magnificent and expansive, while Ightham with its rustic, ramshackle pavilion was a setting like no other. I reckon a decent shove could have just about levelled it, but it continued to serve its purpose and provide a distinctive and striking backdrop, to Saturday and Sunday fixtures alike throughout the season.

Falconhurst was certainly an interesting location, given roaming herds of livestock shared the car park, each one with the capacity to break side mirrors from cars in the blink of an eye.

If any cattle were sighted in the vicinity, the responsibility of chasing them away, would fall to members of the batting team.

The Falconhurst pavilion was as lovely as any and the change rooms, spacious and comfortable. Mind you the playing surface often wasn't the greatest.

I remember batting on a pretty sticky pitch one Sunday, where a bowler's delivery might bounce and reach my waist one minute, only for the following one, of a similar length and speed, to hit me on the toe.

What made Falconhurst special however was an arrangement the club had with its landlord, and the resident of a magnificent, stately mansion that overlooked the cricket ground.

The club rented its facilities, while the owners of the estate remained responsible for the maintenance and upkeep of the pavilion, and its surrounds, which included the cricket ground itself and the pitch.

All of the details of the arrangement were enshrined in a lease document that defined a ninety nine year term, with a ninety nine year option to renew.

The annual rent was a case of claret.

One of the most unique memories I have, of the many 'friendlies' I played, was a mid week T20 game that I was invited to play one evening at Hadlow.

Our team took to the field, with my good friend and Shipbourne team mate, 'Lethal' Lee Morton bowling the first over.

I had been directed to field in the gully and as 'Lethal' sent down the very first delivery of the match, I had the strangest sense of exactly what was about to ensue.

It really was quite bizarre, as everything thereafter seemed to happen in slow motion.

I saw the batsman prop forward and before the ball had even reached him, I was already shifting my (ample) weight to the left.

The ball caught the edge of the bat, just as I appeared to make a full length dive. I fear it was more a case of simple inertia, but I am assured it looked quite impressive all the same.

I extended my left arm as far as I could, as the ball hurtled between me and a slip fielder.

With the back of my hand literally resting on the

grass, I managed to clutch at the ball, wrapping my fingers around it, as I completed the catch.

The batsman shook his head in disbelief, as the bowler and my team mates rushed towards me.

I gratefully accepted their congratulations, then stood up and quite calmly tossed the ball to the wicket keeper, saying 'Right, that's it. It's never going to get any better than that' and walked off the field.

# CHAPTER ELEVEN
## SHIPBOURNE C.C.

As picturesque and wonderful, as many of the cricket grounds that grace the south east of England are, I am not sure any of them could surpass our own.

Shipbourne Cricket Club was accessed via a single gate on Stumble Hill. There was absolutely no signage to indicate the club's location, and the pavilion couldn't be seen from the road.

It was an exclusive cricketing sanctuary, an idyllic oasis, surrounded by Willow trees and bordered by a stream.

The pavilion was single storey, and made of timber. It featured a covered front verandah and inside was a kitchen, shower and toilet, bordered by dressing rooms with wooden benches and windows that presented a view of the ground.

A gas hot water system fuelled the showers, but there was no electricity, which meant plastic milk bottles would rest in a sink filled with cold water prior to the tea break.

A small scoreboard stood to the right of the pavilion, while solid timber bench seats were placed either side of it on match days.

I made a habit of parking my car beneath the same Willow tree each week. It stood tall and proud on the right hand side of the driveway, some distance from the pavilion, but the extra walk allowed me to appreciate the surroundings all the more. Aided by the fact my new Salix kit bag was equipped with wheels.

Maintenance of the outfield and preparation of the pitch was undertaken by club players and volunteers, as were the match day tasks of scoring, and preparation of the tea. Everyone helped to clean up afterwards, with the timber seats neatly stacked away and the pavilion locked, before we made our way to the pub.

Some of the games we played, featured opposition players that spanned three generations, while the range of ages in our own eleven was often quite expansive, particularly if our president turned out to play.

Our president was a very kind and gentle fellow, by the name of Peter Phillips. Or 'Sir Peter' as one wag was in the habit of introducing him to opposition teams.

To the best of my knowledge, the only complaint he ever registered against me, was the fact he could hear my boisterous and ambitious appeals, when bowling, from his home about a mile and a half away, but I did manage to fall foul of him during the annual Estate Game however.

Every year Shipbourne would play a match against a group of employees (and I suspect the odd ring in), of the Fairlawne Estate.

It wasn't a competitive fixture by any means, and one that was seen by the club very much as an opportunity to enhance, and maintain a good relationship with its landlord.

The estate handled all of the catering on the day. It set up marquees and barbecues, while laying on a lavish spread of food, and an abundance of drinks.

I was running late for the game and realising how important a fixture it was to the club, I arrived very much wound up and stressed.

Just as I was dragging my kit bag up the steps leading into the pavilion, I was told that Shipbourne had won the toss, chosen to bat, and that I should 'hurry up and get ready,' as I was opening.

Needless to say, this information did nothing whatsoever to unravel my scrambled state of mind, as I hurriedly donned some whites and changed my shoes, before I attached/inserted all the necessary protective equipment, and scurried out into the middle to face the very first ball of the game.

What immediately followed incurred the president's wrath, as while he was busy 'working the room' beyond the boundary, shaking hands and welcoming our many guests, I managed to slog a pretty innocuous initial delivery over the cover boundary for six.

The bowler looked quite devastated and several heads dropped amongst the fielders, as I could almost hear the president's teeth grinding.

My feeble (if entirely true), excuse was that I was running late and I simply didn't have time to adjust my mind set, and absorb the very relaxed and convivial atmosphere, that others had spent hours creating all morning.

Sorry Sir Peter.

# Chapter Twelve
## The Eagles

An annual fixture, that many of us looked forward to, was our match against the RASRA Eagles.

The Eagles were a roaming club of West Indians, who revelled in re-enforcing the relaxed and celebratory stereotype of the Caribbean.

I am pretty sure that a fair bit of rum was consumed by spectators and players alike (beyond the boundary), as the barracking got louder and the laughter more intense, as the day progressed.

Everyone was caught up in the ensuing mayhem, and I certainly wasn't spared when it came time for me to bat.

One female spectator continued to noisily insist; 'He need more the banana cake!' while others would provide their own specialist commentary and insight when it came to analysing my technique, suggesting; 'He wants to drive, but he ain't got the keys!'

Having compiled a relatively modest score, I was given a rather stern send off by the Eagles' captain, when I missed a pretty friendly full toss, and was trapped leg before wicket.

'Hey man' he said, as I walked off. 'What you doing missing that? You hit that for four every time man' he lamented, pointing to the mid wicket boundary.

Of course the reason I missed it was really quite obvious, and I am surprised he didn't realise it himself.

Not enough banana cake.

# CHAPTER THIRTEEN
## PLAXTOL

Sunday games at Shipbourne were most often but sadly, not always a joy, and I recall one match in particular against Plaxtol, a club that was also a tenant of the Fairlawwne Estate, but located on the far side of the property.

I was slotted to bat at number three and sat outside the pavilion 'padded up,' for what seemed forever, while our opening batsmen compiled a partnership of 178, before one of them was decent enough to get out.

I strode to the crease, nodding hello to one of the fielders, who I knew quite well from my 'Old Oaks' umpiring endeavours, then took guard and prepared to face his fifteen year old son, who was bowling from the top end.

Moments later, I was making a shameful and disconsolate exit, beating a path to the pavilion, having been clean bowled first ball.

A few overs later, I returned to 'the middle,' as part of a regular umpiring rotation. After all, apart from updating the scoreboard, I didn't have much else to do.

I took up a position at the bowler's end, just as my 'Old Oaks' friend, and the proud father was strolling past, a cheeky smile creasing his lips.

'Well you can shut up for a start' I said, as he laughed aloud and walked on.

# CHAPTER FOURTEEN
# THE WITHYHAM CURSE

Withyham Cricket Club was a regular fixture on the Shipbourne Sunday circuit, and enshrined on the Buckhurst Park Estate in East Sussex.

The club was famous for having been used as a film location, for an episode of Doctor Who some years before, having no doubt qualified as an idyllic representation of English village cricket.

If ever there was a cricket ground to rival Shipbourne it was Withyham.

A delightful timber pavilion was set amid a tremendous expanse of lush green pasture, surrounded by trees that were centuries old.

It was almost too big, and the cricket ground itself could have been set in any number of locations on the estate.

Where Shipbourne was subtle and delightful, Withyham was sprawling and boastful, but beautiful all the same.

When it came my turn to bat, I joined my erstwhile running nemesis Ben Spokes, in the middle and I had scored just one run, before I was being audibly identified as a viable run out opportunity by members of the fielding side.

It was loud, rude and sadly accurate, as I was soon on my way back to the pavilion, after an attempted 'quick single,' proved to be more pedestrian in nature.

I don't think there is a worse mode of dismissal in cricket than 'run out,' and I should know. God knows I have managed it often enough.

I returned to the pavilion, with my teammates fearing a minor tantrum was about to ensue, but I simply sighed, said 'One learns to be philosophical about these things,' and then went to buy myself an ice cream.

# CHAPTER FIFTEEN
# HURST GREEN

I was arguably less philosophical one afternoon, later that same season at Hurst Green.

I had opened the batting, and managed to survive for a good couple of hours, with the tea break, and an obligatory declaration fast approaching.

I was starting to think the Cricketing Gods were riding with me that day, as at one point, I even managed to evade a pretty simple run out opportunity, when the wicket keeper dropped a ball that had been thrown from the outfield. The square leg umpire later confirming 'You weren't even in the frame.'

With one over to go before tea, I was on strike, with 98 runs next to my name in the scorebook.

Needless to say, I had six deliveries to score the two runs that I needed to chalk up the first, and probably only, century I would ever make in my entire life.

The bowler sent down a full pitched delivery, that I was able to step forward to, and reach as a half volley. I drove the ball hard and straight, watching it travel inches above the surface of the pitch, and just to the side of the stumps at the far end.

At the time, I thought all it had to do was miss the stumps, and a boundary four was an almost certain outcome.

That was until the bowler reached down, and dived across in his follow through, taking a brilliant one handed catch in the process.

The bowler leapt to his feet, threw the ball high in the air and celebrated wildly with his team mates, as I trudged off the field, stepped into the pavilion and shuffled into the visitors' dressing room.

I leant my bat against a bench and sat down. I wrenched off my pads, threw my gloves on the floor, then stood up and slammed my fist into the wall.

Just my luck, we were playing at the only village cricket ground in Kent that had a brick pavilion.

# Chapter Sixteen
# The Kent League

My first Kent League match as an umpire, was a division two fixture at Whitstable, in a game against Sandwich.

I arrived at the ground and introduced myself to my colleague. We confirmed the playing conditions, got changed in the pavilion, and together invited the captains to toss.

Sandwich won, chose to bat, and within minutes we were underway.

The standard was clearly above the village, school and social fixtures I had umpired the previous year, and I was determined that my own contribution would follow in a similar vein. I channelled my nerves to enhance my concentration, and was just starting to relax into the role, when one of the Sandwich batsmen lifted a ball high over mid on, where it landed amongst the practice nets that were set just beyond the boundary.

I signalled 'six' to the scorers, just as one of the Whitstable fielders called out to me. 'Hang on ump!' he said. 'There's a local rule. That's only four, not six.'

Slightly embarrassed that I hadn't confirmed the specific nuances of the Whitstable venue, I gestured to the scorers, retracted my original signal and confirmed four runs instead of six.

The fielder in question burst out laughing.

I had clearly fallen for the proverbial 'oldest trick in the book,' whereupon I corrected my earlier retraction and restored the original signal.

It was all very good natured and no real harm was done (other than a messy notation in the scorebooks), but I did make a mental note of the player responsible, muttering quietly to myself -'Don't get hit on the pads.'

Everything was progressing well, as I travelled back and forth across the county each Saturday, regaling my Shipbourne team mates, with details of the previous day's play every Sunday.

I umpired matches from Orpington to Canterbury, always grateful for the fact that games were played in a serious and competitive manner, but unfailingly in the right spirit.

With half of the season completed, I was appointed

to my inaugural first division match at Blackheath, in a fixture against Sevenoaks.

My colleague was Neil Kerrison, a very experienced umpire, and one of the 'workplace bullies' that had conducted my oral exam a few months before.

All had been forgiven by this stage however, as I confessed to feeling very nervous about umpiring at first division level.

'It's just another game of cricket' Neil said. 'No different to any other.'

I wish he had been as kind and gracious that Sunday morning in Wateringbury, but his words did resonate, and settle my nerves, all the same.

Blackheath won the toss, chose to bat, and I had the honour of handing Kent contracted player Simon Cook a bowler's marker, so that he could enact the first over.

All of a sudden, my debut in a pre-season village friendly seemed a decade ago.

One the nice aspects of umpiring a number of games in the second division, was that I was able to establish something of a rapport with many of the players. It was all well and good to be considered worthy of a spot in the firsts, but it did mean enacting that process all over again. Rather like being shipped off to a new school I imagine.

All the same, Neil was right. It was just another game of cricket, even if some of the bowlers were a bit faster and some of the batsmen a little more accomplished.

I started to relax and enjoy myself, as despite their best efforts, the game began to slip away from a talented Sevenoaks outfit.

The Blackheath captain had managed to graft his way towards a three figure score, when I heard his opposition counterpart bemoan 'I can't believe a bloke who can't bat is going to get a hundred against us.'

To be fair he had a point. The Blackheath skipper wasn't the most stylish cricketer I had ever seen and he had enjoyed more than an ounce of luck along the way, but he had doggedly resisted and held the bowling attack at bay for the best part of three hours, before reaching a hard earned, and well deserved hundred.

It may well have been crude, but it was certainly effective.

# CHAPTER SEVENTEEN
# THE BEXLEY TEA

The following week I was appointed to another first division game at Bexley.

As far as I could tell, Bexley (rather like Blackheath for that matter), was actually located in London, yet they played in the Kent League.

Geography aside, Bexley was arguably the most kind and generous club I had encountered, among a succession of clubs that were unfailingly kind and generous.

Bexley had a fellow whose responsibility it was to greet the umpires, and escort them to their room in the pavilion. He would offer us both a cup of tea or coffee before the game, ask if there was anything else we needed, and be on hand immediately at the end of the day's play, with our chosen beverage from the bar.

He was also responsible for preparing drinks for the players, having confirmed with the umpires at which point in each innings they would be taken.

I turned up to Bexley one day and was immediately presented with a cup of white coffee, before I was asked, 'Now, what about drinks?'

'I'll have a pint of bitter thanks' I said.

Our host looked at me a little perplexed and embarrassed.

'Actually, I meant for the players' he said.

'Oh, sorry' I said. 'Twenty five overs will do I reckon.'

Teas in the Kent League were tremendous. We even got ice creams at Gore Court, but all the same, no other club could surpass Bexley.

When submitting the match report, Kent League umpires were obliged to grade the tea, giving it a score out of ten, as a trophy was awarded to the winning club at the end of the season.

I think it had been some time since Bexley had actually won the league, but from all reports, the club's name had been engraved on the tea trophy for the past few years in succession.

It was clearly a source of great pride, and little, if any expense or trouble, was spared in its preparation and presentation.

At each home game, Bexley would erect what

effectively became a single, long trestle table, set beneath a crisp, white tablecloth. Each team invariably sat either side of the two umpires, who would sit opposite one another in the middle, as platters of hot pasta, sandwiches, party pies, sausage rolls and mini pizzas were passed back and forth.

I would practically run from the field at the end of a session, and happily round up any stray time to the nearest five minutes, so that we could all derive the maximum benefit from our designated 'half hour' in the pavilion.

For some time now, I have advocated longer tea breaks in one day cricket matches, and if my campaign should ever be successful, I shall consider it 'The Bexley Amendment.'

# Chapter Eighteen
## Decisions, Decisions

My great friend and mentor John Allen once told me 'Umpires don't make mistakes. They make decisions.'

It was a noble sentiment, but not one I ever really embraced, as I continued to adopt a zero tolerance policy to my own failings.

If I became convinced that I had made a mistake, misjudging a run out or failing to detect a faint edge that lead to a caught behind appeal being dismissed, I would stew on it for weeks, losing hours of sleep in the process.

Even so, every so often I was presented with an opportunity to show everyone just how much I knew about the laws of the game, when an obscure or unexpected circumstance occurred.

One such instance happened in the Kent League's T20 finals at Beckenham - an event that drew quite a sizeable crowd.

Two Bexley batsmen had taken a quick single, when a fielder's throw deflected from the stumps at my end, causing one bail to be dislodged, while another remained in place.

The batsmen scurried to secure an overthrow before the bowler caught the subsequent return and with the ball in hand, whipped off the one remaining bail, finding the batsman short of his ground.

I have never been so happy for the meticulous and thorough nature of the training course.

As the incident occurred, in my mind, I could literally see a relevant and corresponding photograph in the text book, one that confirmed the wicket is still considered 'intact,' with just one bail in place.

Needless to say, the batsman saw it differently, but of course he wasn't privy to my comprehensive and detailed education.

Another obscure episode occurred in a game that The Mote was hosting against Lordswood.

A Lordswood bowler sent down a full length delivery, that a Mote batsman jammed down on with his bat.

The ball sat on the surface of the pitch, adjacent to the batsman's feet, before he proceeded to kick it towards mid wicket, and call his partner through for a run.

The relevant law may well have changed since but at the time, the batsman was only allowed to use his bat or any part of his person (not holding the bat), to make a second strike on the ball, for the sole purpose of protecting his wicket. He most certainly had no right to kick it fifty feet, and seek to secure any advantage in so doing.

I was really quite excited at the time, as this was my first, and quite possibly only, opportunity, to ever give a batsman out 'Hit the Ball Twice.'

But no one bloody appealed!

Umpires can only dismiss a batsman after an appeal has been lodged by a member of the fielding side, but all I heard in this instance, was a chorus of 'Hey, he can't do that!'

The most polite and quiet query of 'How's that?' would have sufficed, but nothing eventuated.

My 'Champagne Moment' was ruined. I waited for the batsmen to complete a run, then signalled 'Dead ball' to the scorers, and returned them to their original ends.

Honestly. I don't know why I bother.

# CHAPTER NINETEEN
# THE ONE THAT GOT AWAY

Every so often, I had the opportunity to umpire a game that featured a former international player, and in several instances, I felt quite sure I was umpiring a game that featured a future one.

Maurice Holmes played for Sevenoaks Vine. As a batsman he was a natural number eleven, and in all honesty, I reckon he would have been just as effective had he faced up holding his bat at the wrong end.

Needless to say, Maurice wasn't in the team for his batting, he was in the team because he was the most prodigious bowling talent that I (and I dare say several others), had ever seen.

An old boy of Tonbridge, he had only decided to try his hand at cricket after he left school, deciding to give the spin bowling caper a go.

At the time, Tonbridge School employed a former Zimbabwean international off spinner as a coach, but perhaps Maurice benefited from being spared the formalities of a structured coaching regimen.

However it came about, Maurice Holmes managed to develop a unique bowling action and mode of delivery, that together, allowed him to deliver a cricket ball that could vary in pace and flight, while bouncing and deviating sharply from the surface of the pitch, in just about any direction.

In short, he was a gifted off spin bowler who could deliver a vicious leg break and all without any discernible difference in his bowling action.

I can remember umpiring a game at Hartley Cricket Club, where I overheard one of the Hartley players mourn the fact that their captain (a former England all rounder), looked liked Ray Charles when facing him.

I was convinced Maurice would play for England, and I contacted a number of online and corporate bookmakers, hoping to secure a huge price that one day he indeed would.

None of them obliged, and I decided to settle for the bragging rights, as and when he did.

In the meantime, I would spruik him as 'the next big thing,' to anyone who would listen and continued to follow his performances and career with great interest.

He took a mid season break from playing with Sevenoaks, after being hit by a car while at university, and again the following season when he was offered a contract with Warwickshire. Former England off spinner Ashley Giles was Warwickshire's head coach at the time, and he had clearly seen tremendous potential in the skinny kid from Kent.

Why he wasn't snapped up by his own county remains a mystery.

I believe Maurice sent down a number of deliveries to Kent captain Rob Key, having been invited to a training session at Canterbury, whereupon Key is said to have finished his stint, walked out of the nets and said 'Sign him up,' to whomever was in charge.

Maurice certainly had a unique bowling action, the legitimacy of which some people had questioned, and I was very sad to hear some years later that he had been banned from bowling by the governing body for cricket in England - a decision that some former players, and television commentators have since openly criticised.

Why those in charge didn't invest the necessary time and money to work with him and modify his action, to address any issues, simply baffles me.

I have since seen a profile photo of Maurice on

social media that shows him swinging a golf club. Perhaps he will win the British Open one day. But he won't be winning 'The Ashes' for England any time soon, that's for sure and even as a proud and passionate Australian, I think that's a crying shame.

# CHAPTER TWENTY
# COATS ON, COATS OFF

My third season of umpiring in the Kent League, was given a wonderful endorsement, when I was asked to umpire a County 2nd XI match, between Kent and Sussex.

Such matches were normally the domain of umpires appointed to the ECB's Reserve List, a second tier of top level umpires (many of whom were former First Class players), who were intent on making cricket umpiring a career, and needless to say, hoping to advance further to the first class list and beyond.

I am not sure just how my name came into the mix, and to be honest I didn't much care, as I cleared three days in the diary the following week, to stand in a game at Mote Park in Maidstone.

A three day game would prove something of a marathon for me, as to date, I had only stood in one day matches in the Kent League.

Excited as I was about the opportunity, I wasn't all that disappointed to see that showers were forecast for much of the week, as a few breaks in play might at least give my feet a rest.

I arrived at Mote Park and met my colleague. He was a very experienced umpire who was well known to both teams, and someone to whom I continued to defer when it came time to discuss just when play should start, stop and re-commence.

The standard wasn't all that far above the Kent League's first division. In fact, I already knew two or three of the Kent players, but by the same token, most of those involved were professional cricketers, who were contracted to their county, and no doubt hoping to secure a spot in their respective 1st XI teams.

Rain interrupted play a number of times on the first day in particular, and we seemed to spend as much time in the pavilion as we did in the middle, which lead to a minor faux pas on my part.

With all of the players sitting inside and anxiously looking out onto the field, I returned from the umpires' room wearing my white Kent League umpire's jacket, whereupon a surprised Sussex captain asked me 'Are we going out?'

'No' I replied.

'But you've got your jacket on' he said.

'Well I'm cold' I fired back, not realising that in the professional ranks, umpires donning jackets is an indication that they expected play to shortly re-commence.

Unlike my colleague, I didn't have a branded ECB off field uniform, and I spent the next hour or so feeling uncomfortably chilly, while we waited for the skies to clear.

I returned the following day having packed a plain, navy blue fleece, which spent most of the day in my bag, as we spent most of the day on the field.

I was getting on well with the players and captains and while the tone of the game was competitive and at times a little edgy, it was generally played in a good spirit.

It was of course a two innings match, and seeing some of the Kent batsmen return in the second innings was certainly a novelty.

We had lost almost a third of the designated playing time due to rain however, and it was clear from shortly after the lunch break on the third day that the match was destined to finish in a tame draw.

All the same, it was a great experience, a lot of fun, and an opportunity I was tremendously grateful for, even if I did catch a cold in the process.

# Chapter Twenty One
# Sign Here Please

One of the many great aspects about umpiring in the Kent League, was the opportunity to meet any number of First Class and International players.

Niall O'Brien was one of them, and we crossed paths when he was playing with Folkestone, shortly after keeping wicket for Ireland at the World Cup.

He was a talented player but an annoying commentator, as he felt obliged to keep us all constantly informed of his opinions and strategies from behind the stumps.

I was well tired of the constant chatter, to say nothing of his high pitched voice and piercing accent, when I decided to enact a small measure of revenge.

Knowing full well how precious wicket keepers can be when it comes to extras recorded against their name in the score book, I seized upon an opportunity when he was standing up to the stumps.

A bowler's delivery had clearly brushed the batsman's pad, before crossing the boundary for four runs, when I turned to the non striker and said 'Watch this.'

I turned around, faced the pavilion and signalled to the scorers with a raised open palm, secure in the knowledge they would record four 'byes' in the score book and pretty much ruin O'Brien's day.

It certainly had the desired effect, as he spent the next few minutes kicking at the turf and protesting the decision to anyone who would listen. I was branded a 'Feckin eejit' for my trouble, but considered it a clear points victory all the same.

The following year I had a phone call quite out of the blue. It was from a very well spoken fellow whose name I didn't recognise and I slouched in my chair, fearing he was about to pitch me some elaborate investment scheme.

'I'm from Kent County Cricket Club' he said, as I sharply sat bolt upright.

Apparently Kent had arranged to play two pre-season practice matches against Nottinghamshire and Northamptonshire and they needed an umpire.

No prizes for guessing the outcome of that conversation.

I arrived at the St. Lawrence ground in Canterbury to

be greeted by Ken Amos, who was the head of the Kent League umpires' panel and three of my team mates from Shipbourne, who had taken the day off work to watch.

Both teams comprised a handful of internationals and I was absolutely thrilled to be involved, particularly as I got to sign my very first (and to date only), autograph for a young boy who had secured a prime position outside the dressing rooms.

The captains didn't toss, but instead reached a mutual agreement as to which team would bat first and for how long. It was decided that Notts would bat for the first day of the game and Kent the second.

The atmosphere both on and off the field was pretty casual and over time I relaxed into the role.

I even managed to share a nice moment with Kent's Darren Stevens, when he was bowling from my end.

Kent wicket keeper and erstwhile Ashes hero, Geraint Jones, was standing up to the stumps, when a Nottinghamshire batsman played at a delivery that continued to travel past his wicket.

Stevens launched into a raucous appeal for caught behind, before realising that Jones had in fact fumbled the ball and dropped the 'catch.'

The keeper then did his best to convince the bowler that the ball had not in fact hit the edge of the bat, but rather that it had flicked the batsman's pad.

Stevens look largely unconvinced, as he turned around and walked back to his mark.

As he passed me, I turned towards him and said 'Ah, we'll never know.'

Rather sportingly, he smiled and replied 'No, we'll never know.'

I returned a week later for the match against Northamptonshire, and met Ken again in the umpires' room on the first level of the grandstand.

'There you go' he said, pointing to the back page of a local newspaper that he had hung on the wall, courtesy of a coat hook.

I read the headline, and the first few paragraphs of an article that clearly related to the Notts' game the week before.

'So? What of it?' I said.

'The photo' he replied.

I diverted my focus to a large colour photograph of Kent's opening bowler Robbie Joseph, sending down a delivery the week before. Behind him, stood the figure of a very tall umpire, wearing a white coat, a broad brimmed hat and an Australian MCC member's tie. His gaze was fixed with the most earnest concentration.

'Oh it's me!' I said excitedly.

# CHAPTER TWENTY TWO
## TIME

Another cricket season had ended and as much as I was looking forward to the next one, circumstances dictated that I would almost certainly return to Australia in the New Year.

I was very anxious to continue my umpiring role, and given I would be returning to Melbourne, I studied the Cricket Victoria web site, in search of an appropriate contact who might help me to facilitate just that.

Bob Parry was the Umpiring Manager, and I composed an email that outlined my qualifications and experience, in the hope that an opportunity might present itself in Victoria's Premier Cricket competition.

Bob was kind enough to reply quite promptly, and he suggested that I give him a call when I was back in the country, so we could arrange to meet.

In the meantime, I kept my 'eye in' umpiring a six

a side indoor cricket competition, that was held once a week, on a basketball court, at a secondary school in Seal, a small village a few minutes from Sevenoaks.

I knew most of the players and other umpires from the Kent League and local village ranks, while we played with a white coloured ball, that comprised the usual leather outer, encasing what I am assured, was the rubber inner of a tennis ball.

The pitch measured more or less a normal length, but the bowlers' run ups were restricted to just a few metres, and the batsmen only had to cover half the length of the pitch to complete a run.

Games were played on Sunday afternoons (usually three or four in succession), with umpires rotating throughout, and occasionally being 'rung in,' if any teams turned up short of numbers.

On one occasion, I had the inestimable pleasure of carting my umpiring colleague Ian Fraser's leg spin all over the court, when we were each drafted to fill in for opposing teams.

Granted, it was impossible for him to divert the path of a cricket ball from a polished wood surface, and the bloke was probably in his sixties at the time, but it still counts!

Shipbourne entered a team each week and we

would all convene at the Five Bells in Seal for a few pints afterwards.

As we sat by the fire, drinking, laughing and playing a derivation of cricket on the dart board, it started to dawn on me what I would be leaving behind, once I flew back to Australia.

I count myself tremendously lucky that I stumbled upon the opportunity to umpire, and play cricket (after a twenty year absence from the game), and all because some tree hit the deck, forty odd miles away.

I would miss everything about cricket in England.

I would miss its history and traditions, together with the beautiful grounds that populated towns, villages and the odd private estate in the south east of the country. To say nothing of my colleagues, team mates, opponents and players.

My Shipbourne team mates used to think I was a bit odd, as we would often arrive at a new venue, only for me to get excited about the pavilion, the trees and the grass, even the scoreboard, fences and boundary markers.

Although to be fair, waxing lyrical about boundary markers was probably a bit much.

I loved the post match beer, and I would miss the pubs. They were unique and special. Village pubs in

England were the fabric that bound communities together, fostering friendships and ties that would last a lifetime.

I would miss umpiring and I would miss playing, but above all, I would miss my friends.

# CHAPTER TWENTY THREE
# MY SECOND FIRST SEASON

I returned to Melbourne in February and soon after, travelled to Toorak Park one Saturday afternoon, to see both the Prahran 1st XI and umpires in action.

I didn't rate the umpires' uniform much. Both officials were dressed in tan coloured long sleeved shirts, that would have looked a bit below par in the seventies, while the standard issue, broad brim white hats and black trousers were retained.

I thought about introducing myself, as they left the field for an innings break, but I figured they would probably have enough to do as it is, and I didn't dare assume that I would become their colleague the following season anyway.

I contacted Bob Parry again the following week and he suggested that we meet for a coffee in the MCG's Hugh Trumble Cafe, which proved to be a short walk from the Cricket Victoria offices in Jolimont.

We confirmed my experience and qualifications and Bob assured me that he would be only too happy for me to join the Premier Cricket umpires' panel, subsequent to me attending a series of winter classes, and successfully completing an exam.

I wasn't too thrilled at having to repeat a process that I had enacted a few years before, but it was when he suggested that he would start me off in the 3$^{rd}$ XI competition, that I just about choked on my latte.

'Well that would be great' I said, lying through my teeth, all the while realising there was no point in debating the issue.

A few months later, I showed up at the Holmesglen TAFE in Warrigal Road, where several of us sat in a lecture theatre, being instructed about the laws of the game, by a number of experienced Premier Cricket umpires.

After six weeks I was given the opportunity to sit a written exam.

Apparently I passed but I have never been given a grade, a mark or any indication of just how I did. In fact no one did.

Such information was considered confidential, and it would remain the sole property of the Cricket Victoria umpiring department.

The umpiring department consisted of two people, both of whom shared an office, that on the original floor plan was probably defined as a closet.

Bob's assistant was responsible for guarding the exam results, and when I suggested that if an umpire made a mistake in an exam, surely he or she was likely to do the same thing at some point in a match, he failed to embrace the logic.

Curiously, the same fellow would berate umpires at meetings for making errors and omissions in match reports, citing the importance of 'attention to detail,' when I can't recall a single email he ever sent members of the panel, that he didn't have to retract or subsequently correct, having made an error himself.

My application to join the Premier Cricket umpires' panel was successful and I was invited to attend a pre-season seminar at the Junction Oval in St. Kilda, where various elements, such as playing conditions would be confirmed and uniforms allocated.

I was one of about twelve new inductees, and relieved to see that the on field umpiring shirt for the new season would in fact be coloured light blue and not light brown.

# CHAPTER TWENTY FOUR
# MY SECOND FIRST GAME

I was appointed to my first game soon after. It was a 3rd XI one day fixture between Essendon and Footscray, to be played on a Saturday at Cross Keys Reserve.

To say that Cross Keys was a far cry from any of the village and league grounds where I had umpired and played in Kent, would be the understatement of all time.

The outfield was dry, parched and sparsely grassed. The pavilion consisted of two makeshift change rooms, while the umpires' room itself was a shipping container.

Worse still, Cross Keys was the site of two recent gangland murders, where career criminal Jason Moran was gunned down, together with his bodyguard, by an underworld contemporary, while sitting in his car.

Apparently he was watching his young son take part in an AFL AusKick clinic during the football season, before his car, together with its two occupants, was riddled with bullets.

And from all reports, nobody saw a thing.

Delightful.

John Allen had appointed me to Meopham for my very first umpiring assignment, owing to its long association with the Melbourne Cricket Club. I have no doubt he knew how much I would appreciate it.

It seemed to me as if Bob Parry had appointed me to Cross Keys for my first match in Victoria, just to see how long I would last.

My colleague was Jeff Diamond-Smith. He was a very friendly, jovial fellow and we established a good relationship from the outset.

Jeff had a few seasons under his belt and during the week he worked with the tax office, which given I hadn't lived in the country for the past ten years, didn't particularly faze me.

The game hadn't been underway for very long, when it became clear that club cricket in Victoria was a very different animal.

The venue itself (without wanting to be too unkind), was a dump and many of the players conducted themselves in a manner that seemed to embrace that.

Perhaps it was simply a reflection of their surroundings, but much of the game was played in an edgy and narky fashion, with any number of nasty and biting remarks traded throughout.

Mind you, this was merely a dress rehearsal for what was to follow.

# CHAPTER TWENTY FIVE
# FRANKSTON

Several weeks later, I was appointed to a one day 3rd XI semi final at Frankston, in a match against Geelong.

Frankston won the toss and chose to bat.

I have no recollection of how many runs they scored, as I have since done all I can to erase any memory of the entire game, but I don't think it was many.

Frankston came out to bowl, and as I later explained to a senior official at Cricket Victoria, they didn't set about dismissing or restricting Geelong as a cricket team, so much as a pack of wild dogs.

From the outset, Frankston players were constantly shouting, clapping and doing everything they could to distract and annoy their opponents.

The Geelong players each had their surnames printed on the back of their shirts, which only served to give

Frankston more ammunition to fire off, with an endless array of spiteful remarks and interpretations regarding their ancestry. None of which were the least bit clever, funny or imaginative.

With the game slipping away, the Frankston captain directed an off spin bowler, to take up the attack (literally) from my end.

Early in the over, a Geelong batsman stepped out of his crease and lofted a delivery over mid wicket for four runs.

When he tried to repeat the stroke from the bowler's subsequent offering, he could only edge the ball into his pad.

That prompted the Frankston bowler to march down the middle of the pitch, while shouting at his opponent 'You fucking spastic!'

I then strode down the middle of the pitch myself, pointing a grave and accusing finger at the bowler, saying 'Right. You're being reported!'

The bowler stood to the side of the pitch, with his arms outstretched in utter bemusement as to why.

'What for?!' he shouted.

I called his captain and my colleague over, and as the bowler continued to protest his innocence, I told him 'I am not even going to repeat what you said.'

I was absolutely livid, very upset and struggling to maintain a degree of detachment, when his captain asked me 'Is that just a warning?'

'No it is not just a warning' I said sternly, 'he is being reported.'

I never really paid that much attention to reporting procedures and the completion of relevant forms during our pre-season seminar, but with the help of my colleague, we managed to get it all done and ensure that everything was lodged correctly.

At the time, umpires had the option of simply ticking a box on a form that would recommend a one match suspension for any player they reported, which the player charged could later dispute (if he wished), by asking to plead his case at a tribunal hearing.

I refused to tick any of the boxes on any of the forms and by email that evening, insisted that Cricket Victoria arrange a tribunal hearing during the week, 'so it could make an example of the individual concerned and his club.'

The tribunal convened a few days later on a Tuesday evening.

My colleague and I arrived, each wearing our navy blue (off field uniform), Cricket Victoria Umpire polo shirts.

The individual charged, arrived wearing football shorts and a pair of thongs, or flip flops as I came to know them in the UK.

My colleague and I were asked to present our evidence, as to what occurred where and when, who did what, and who said what to whom.

Having established the fact that I was positioned a metre or so behind the stumps at the bowler's end, the tribunal chairman (who I had been assured was an experienced barrister), asked me what was quite possibly the dumbest question I have ever entertained.

'Could it be heard beyond the boundary?' he said.

I resisted the urge to say 'Well, how the hell would I know?' and simply confirmed that as I was standing some seventy metres from the boundary at the time, that I really wasn't in position to say, nor was I in a position (in the middle of a game) to wander around beyond the fence, taking a survey of spectators, players and officials, asking what (if anything), any of them had heard.

Having given our evidence, my colleague and I were asked to leave, while I imagine the tribunal questioned the offender further, and deliberated on an appropriate penalty.

Personally, I would give him two matches for the

shorts, two for the thongs and six for the offence.

In four years umpiring in the Kent League, I had occasion to report one player, who committed a serious but all the same, arguably lesser offence. He received a four match suspension from the league, and his club told him to pack his bags and never return.

No one from Cricket Victoria bothered to contact me the following day (nor since), to say 'Thank you' for travelling the best part of three hours to and from the tribunal hearing, and I have never received any official advice as to the outcome of the tribunal's deliberations.

I did hear some weeks later however (from another umpire), that the individual concerned had been suspended for one match.

Ever since, I have been waiting for the opportunity to raise my hand at a meeting and question a member of the Cricket Victoria Tribunal thus;

'If you are going to shout 'You fucking spastic!' at an opponent, then turn up at a tribunal wearing shorts and thongs, to get suspended for one match. What do you have to do to get two?'

# CHAPTER TWENTY SIX
## NATURAL SELECTION

Before the start of the following season, I wrote an email to Umpiring Manager Bob Parry. I said that I was very grateful for the opportunity to umpire Premier Cricket matches in Victoria, but that I hadn't enjoyed the experience to anything like the degree I had in England.

The exception for me, had been the handful of women's matches I had umpired during the season, and that if it was at all possible, I would like to remain on the panel, but umpire Women's Premier Cricket matches exclusively.

I feared a rather stern email would follow in reply, the likes of 'Listen son, you go where we send you, or you don't go anywhere at all' but the fact is I never received a reply.

I decided that if Bob didn't grant my request, I would effectively retire, at least until I had the opportunity to return to England one day.

Feeling somewhat 'in limbo,' I showed up for the winter classes once again, as Cricket Victoria continued to insist that all panel umpires attend every year.

Bob was standing behind a table where all those present were asked to confirm their attendance, by signing their names on a printed roll.

When he saw me approach he greeted me warmly. He confirmed that he had received my email and that my request was perfectly fine with him.

From that moment on I have to date, been the only member of the Cricket Victoria Premier umpires' panel to stand in Women's Premier Cricket matches exclusively.

Why others have yet to follow suit, I have no idea.

The previous season I stood in three Women's 2nd XI fixtures and one 1st XI match, which Cricket Victoria's own administration and web site recorded as the equivalent of three 4th XI matches, and one 2nd XI match.

The supposed 2nd XI equivalent included three Victorian players and an Australian representative, who had just returned from the T20 World Cup in Sri Lanka.

The grades didn't particularly bother me, but I thought the players deserved better.

At one point during the season, I had umpired the Dandenong 2nd XI two weeks in succession, the first in an away fixture at Casey Fields, and the second when they were playing a home game at Greaves Reserve.

Towards the end of the second game, a young Dandenong captain asked me if I would be umpiring all of their games from now on.

I explained that umpires were actually appointed week to week, and that I doubted it very much.

'Oh' she said, looking rather disappointed. 'You're such a good umpire. We really like you.'

Who wouldn't want that?

## CHAPTER TWENTY SEVEN
## THE FOOD CHAIN

With the possible exception of scorers, umpires are located pretty much at the bottom of the cricketing hierarchy. Most continue in the role because they love the game, they want to remain involved and they enjoy making a contribution.

Very few umpire for recognition, or financial reward.

From the perspective of the governing authorities, umpires are almost an afterthought, regarded as a necessary evil and an inconvenient expense.

From the perspective of the people immediately in charge of those same umpires however, nothing could be further from the truth.

Time and again, at meetings both before and during the season, umpires were told that Victoria's Premier Cricket competition was 'the best and most elite club cricket competition in the world,' and that as members of the Premier Cricket umpires' panel, we were the best of the best, an elite and privileged band of individuals who were firmly positioned at the very top of the umpiring profession.

Anyone who had occasion to wander into one of our meetings, could be forgiven for thinking that cricket umpiring was just about the most important, and valuable vocation, that anyone could ever hope to pursue.

During my time, the umpires' panel has included orthopaedic surgeons, commercial pilots, IT consultants, accountants and teachers. Which is all well and good, but what really mattered, was the fact we were all Premier Cricket umpires.

The sad thing is some of us actually seemed to believe it.

I remember spending one rather long day in the field with an experienced colleague, who took every opportunity to remind me of the various Sheffield Shield and BBL matches he had umpired, having earlier offered to stay behind after the game, if there was anything I wanted to ask him.

'You can squeeze me like a sponge' he said.

The start of the match was delayed, as there were areas of the square that were still damp after rain had fallen the previous day and overnight.

As we were speaking to the groundsman, who was busily preparing the pitch, my colleague pointed out some of the water that was gathering on the surface of the roller.

'Can you see that moisture on the roller there?' he said. 'That's because the side of the pitch is wet.'

Gee. Thanks professor.

# CHAPTER TWENTY EIGHT
# THE BEST OF THE BEST

Cricket Victoria umpires are often asked to give up their time during the week, over the duration of the school holidays, to umpire a series of Pathway or Youth Premier League games, that consist of various underage teams, representing any number of metropolitan and country regions around the state.

It is a terrific concept and one that I, and many others, are only too happy to support.

All the same, the attraction dulled somewhat for me, at my very first mid-week appointment.

I wandered into the pavilion at Dendy Park in Brighton during a lunch break, to see a plethora of sandwiches and drinks laid out for the players and their coaches.

I hadn't even closed the door behind me, before I was told, in no uncertain terms, to leave by a uniformed Cricket Victoria employee, who stood in my path and waved me away, saying 'There's nothing for you here.'

Fortunately, I had some cash in the car and there was a cafe nearby, where I met up with a couple of colleagues and purchased my own lunch.

Since then, invitations have been sent to umpires each year, asking them to give up their time during the week, and contribute to Youth Premier League games for a modest fee. Each email confirmed that umpires were expected to bring their own lunch.

Bob Parry had moved on to a position at Cricket Australia, before I called into the office one day, to meet with his replacement and original assistant.

I had been asked to stand in a handful of mid week school games, and I wanted to pick up a couple of white umpiring shirts that were part of an earlier season's uniform, so that I could be similarly attired to my colleague.

No sooner had I entered the building, than a girl standing behind the reception desk recognised me and said 'You must be here to see Bert and Ernie.'

Is that any way to treat the best of the best?

# Chapter Twenty Nine
# No one is ever out LBW

I love umpiring Women's Premier Cricket matches, and I have said many times over the years, that if it was down to me, I would schedule all of the 1st XI fixtures on different days of the week, and umpire each and every one.

Loathe as I am, to make sweeping generalisations about the women's game, there is one aspect I simply cannot refute however.

No one is ever out leg before wicket.

It's as if the law came into to effect during the week, and no one got the memo.

This aspect was never more colourfully illustrated than in the very first Women's 1st XI match that I umpired - a fixture between Dandenong and Brunswick Park.

This was of course prior to Brunswick Park briefly becoming Brunswick, before later merging with Prahran.

The match had been relocated to a venue in Chadstone, as an industrial dispute between ground staff and the Dandenong Council had meant a pitch wasn't prepared at Greaves Reserve.

Brunswick Park won the toss, chose to bat and their two 'big guns' in Elyse Villani and Emma Inglis came out to open the innings.

Dandenong responded in kind, with their Australian representative seamer Julie Hunter, opening the bowling from my end.

In the third over of the game (Hunter's second), Villani stepped forward and with bended knee and a raised bat, she aimed to escort a delivery that had pitched outside of her off stump through to the wicket keeper.

What she didn't anticipate was just how much and how late the ball would swing, before it thudded into her pad.

A huge appeal followed from the bowler, wicket keeper, slips cordon and just about every fielder within ear shot.

The ball had struck Villani's pad outside the line of the stumps, well below the knee roll and after careful consideration and deliberation, together with the fact she had clearly made no attempt to hit the ball with her bat, I concluded that had she not put her leg in the way, the ball would have otherwise hit the stumps.

I raised my arm, extended an index finger and gave her out.

What followed was at the very least unnerving, if not rather frightening.

Villani said nothing but clenched her jaw, gritted her teeth and stared at me with a disdainful, angry glare. In short, it looked like she wanted to kill me, and for a moment I felt very exposed, given she had a pretty sizeable and effective weapon at her disposal, while all I was armed with was a plastic ball counter and a bowling card.

To her credit however, and to my lasting relief, she soon turned around, tucked her bat under her arm and walked off.

Some five hours later, Brunswick Park had won the game, whereupon it was time for players and umpires to shake hands.

When it came time for Elyse to shake mine, she gave me the death stare once again, her eyes drilling fiercely into my own.

I can't imagine what might have happened had her team lost.

For the record, I think Elyse Villani is a wonderful cricketer. She is a World Cup winner with Australia, and a dynamic, athletic and powerful player into the bargain. She is clearly very well liked and respected by her teammates and in the few times we have cross paths and spoken since, she has always been very polite, respectful and friendly.

But boy she can hold a grudge.

# Chapter Thirty
## The Julie Bishop Award

At the end of each season, and entirely for my own amusement, I type up a list of awards that I 'present' to players who have performed the most impressive and spectacular feats, in specific categories. Best shot, best catch, best delivery and so on, even best appeal for that matter.

The Gold Logie equivalent is of course the Julie Bishop Award. That's the one presented to the girl who gave me the filthiest look for giving her out LBW during the course of the season, and there are no prizes for guessing whose name was first engraved on the trophy.

One year the award was shared. Not by two players as you might expect, but by one Box Hill player and her mother.

The player concerned was an established star at her club and a rising one within the Victorian ranks and those of the Melbourne Stars.

She was still at school when her team won through to the Girls Sport Victoria Senior Cricket Final, an event that was played one mid week afternoon at Basil Reserve in East Malvern.

Mark Hanton, a fellow Premier Cricket umpire was charged with the responsibility of umpiring the final, and he was kind enough to invite me to accompany him.

We had a pre-match discussion with both schools' coaches and all of us agreed that the LBW law would apply throughout course of the match, despite the fact it had apparently been dispensed with, in all of the competition's matches leading up to the final.

It all made perfect sense to me and the four of us were certainly on the same page.

If only the coaches had bothered to tell their captains.

The player in question strode to the crease wearing a Cricket Victoria Academy helmet, and proceeded to club the first ball of the game through the covers for four.

When the bowler sent down her second delivery, the striker planted her foot in front of the stumps and swung across the line of the ball, aiming to despatch it across, or possibly over the mid wicket boundary.

The ball thudded into her pad, without making any contact with her bat and she was soon on her way.

In a club game later that season she glared at me repeatedly, and when I enquired as to why, she confirmed that she was still upset about the GSV final decision.

I tried to explain that we had agreed the LBW law would apply, in a pre-match conference with both coaches, when she pointed out (quite correctly to be fair), that we hadn't ourselves, told the captains.

I apologised and asked her what sort of time frame we might be looking at, before she might find it in her heart to forgive me, suggesting a period of weeks or even months.

'Never' she replied.

I suggested that we should put the entire episode behind us, and that we needed to move on.

She didn't buy it.

Not long after, I returned to umpire another 1st XI fixture at Box Hill.

It was a bright, sunny day with a gentle breeze, and soon after arriving, I wandered into the pavilion to greet the scorers and officials.

I announced to everyone present, how much I was

looking forward to the game, and that I thought it would be a great match.

There was a small group of what were clearly parents standing close by, and one woman immediately broke ranks to suggest (quite ferociously), that it might indeed be a great game, if I didn't give her daughter out LBW again.

Of course, it wouldn't be a game of cricket if I didn't upset someone, but by the same token, we usually manage to get things underway before I do.

# CHAPTER THIRTY ONE
## BOX HILL

Box Hill has been one of the most successful women's cricket clubs in the Premier competition in recent years, despite the fact they have no affiliation with an established Men's Premier Cricket club.

They play their home games at the City Oval, also home to the Box Hill Hawks in the Victorian Football League, which presents their groundsmen with something of a challenge, when it comes to preparing cricket pitches for the first few rounds of the season.

The club was well and truly established before I arrived on the scene, and it was clear to me from the outset, that Box Hill had an enviable junior development and coaching structure, as even their youngest players (many of whom were coming through the ranks of the Victorian Women's Community Cricket competition), had developed very sound techniques early in their careers, and were demonstrating a solid grasp of the game.

Box Hill is also home (when state, national and WBBL fixtures allow), to the Australian captain and one of the best female cricketers in the world in Meg Lanning.

Lanning has a unique capacity to treat a club game with just as much focus, concentration and intensity as any international fixture.

From the moment she steps onto the field, she is out there to win, and she while she can certainly appreciate that most of her team mates don't possess anything like her ability, she does expect they will follow her example when it comes to focus, concentration and commitment.

While in the field, and even occasionally bowling, she is always reluctant to accept an umpire's call of 'wide,' often responding with a clear and audible response of her own.

'Really?!' is an expression I have heard more than once, knowing full well that it is in fact code for 'What are you blind?!'

Our most memorable confrontation came in a game against Essendon Maribyrnong Park, when Lanning herself was fielding at silly mid on.

She took up a position adjacent to the pitch, just

ahead of the batting crease, which meant the non striker would have to back up and run a few metres wider that she might normally.

The over was progressing perfectly well, until she crouched in her position, then stepped across and placed her left foot onto the surface of the pitch, just as the bowler released the ball.

By law, that is a 'No ball' and I called and signalled exactly that.

Just as I had finished indicating that a 'Free hit' would follow, the bowler returned, enquiring as to the nature of the infringement.

'Front foot?' she asked.

'Not yours, Meg's' I replied.

What followed was a wildly disproportionate reaction from the captain, as she expressed her obvious displeasure and absolute disbelief at the decision, and where I did my best to explain why it was in fact a 'No ball.'

In the end, I suggested that she should contact the MCC, if she wanted to seek any clarification, or have the law changed, but for now, perhaps we could just get on with the game.

To be fair, I think umpires need to be mindful of the fact, that Meg Lanning is a unique talent, and there is a reason why she has reached the level she has. She is one of the most driven, determined and intensely focussed people I have ever met.

I had the pleasure of umpiring her in a game that Box Hill played against Plenty Valley the following season.

Box Hill won the toss, chose to bat and soon after, Meg strode out to open the batting with her sister Anna.

Some time later, Anna Lanning was out for 85, she and her sister having compiled 218 for their opening partnership.

The score had reached 380 before Meg herself was out, only just failing to carry her bat throughout her team's 50 over allocation.

Her own total of 244 (from 145 balls, with 39 fours and 2 sixes) was itself a record, eclipsing the 241 not out that she had accumulated a few years before, in Melbourne's inaugural season.

I don't often write much as an addendum to match reports, but in this instance I thought Box Hill's opposition deserved the following recognition;

*The entire Plenty Valley team is to be congratulated and commended for their conduct and attitude during the Box Hill innings. They never gave up, they adopted an enthusiastic and energetic approach throughout, while there was never a cross word or snide remark to be heard at any stage.*

*The Plenty Valley captain and her players truly embodied the spirit, nature and traditions of the game.*

Meg Lanning aside, Box Hill is invariably a talented and committed outfit, with as much depth in its ranks as any side in the league and the best afternoon teas in the competition.

While the club is yet to reach the sort of heights that Bexley achieved in the Kent League, when it comes to Women's Premier Cricket, Box Hill takes the cake. Pun intended.

One of the nice aspects of umpiring a competition that comprises just eight teams, is the opportunity it presents to get to know captains and players better, and more quickly than I otherwise might.

As a consequence, I suspect some players may have been a little more forgiving of perceived (and probable) errors, on my part.

I remember dismissing a run out appeal at the bowler's end one afternoon, when then Box Hill captain Anna Lanning shook her head rather miserably, making it quite clear (as did a couple of others), that she thought the striker's bat was in the air, when the wicket was broken and before the run was completed.

I could argue that being 6ft 5in tall, that perhaps my depth perception was impaired, but the reality is I almost certainly made a mistake.

A couple of overs later, Box Hill's Cassie Brock managed to clean bowl the same girl, with a delivery that was released and flighted with tremendous precision.

Moments later, I returned the ball to the bowler, as she was mid conference with her captain and a team mate.

'Well, that's me out of gaol then' I said, soliciting smiles all round.

# CHAPTER THIRTY TWO
# CARLTON BRUNSWICK

Carlton Brunswick is one the newer clubs inducted into the first division of Women's Premier Cricket, and in the short time they have been involved they have become a competitive outfit.

In the few games I have umpired at their home ground, they were responsible for one of the most unique reasons for the umpires to suspend play.

The weather was fine, it wasn't particularly hot and a gentle breeze was wafting across the ground, having passed through a row of tall Pine trees growing beyond the boundary as it did.

Carlton Brunswick were bowling and I was standing at the striker's end, when I became quite confused and distracted by a faint and constant humming noise, that seemed to be emanating from the trees on the other side of the ground.

I couldn't understand just what it was and tried to

put it out of my mind and concentrate on the job at hand, just as a couple of fielders on the far side of the pitch dived onto the ground.

Moments later, they were lying face down and trying to make themselves appear as inconspicuous as possible.

The reason and culprit, was a large swarm of bees that had perhaps hitherto made their home in the nearby trees, only to decide that today was a good day to check out some of the alternative accommodation options that the neighbourhood offered.

My colleague and I wandered across, wondering if perhaps the 'invasion' consisted of just a handful of insects, before we bid a hasty retreat ourselves, suspending play immediately and appropriately enough, making a bee line for the pavilion.

Anxious as everyone was for play to recommence, no one was all that keen to conduct a thorough and detailed inspection of the ground, least of all me, but there was little choice other than for my colleague and me to step up and do just that.

We ventured out and came back two or three times, before deciding that the threat had subsided and having taken a quick straw poll, asking if any players from either side had any known allergies, we managed to re-commence play and complete the match without further incident.

Another memorable game was a mid week T20 match where Carlton Brunswick was drawn to play at Dandenong's Wilson Oval - a venue that was located just outside the Panther's main ground.

The timing of the fixture had been engineered to accommodate a number of interstate and overseas players, who had been enlisted to play with one of the two Melbourne based franchises in the Women's Big Bash League.

Such players were in turn inducted into the ranks of various Premier Cricket clubs (possibly for the first and only time in their entire career), as a means of securing some valuable match practice, before the WBBL competition kicked off.

On that score, I have to acknowledge and congratulate Queensland based Australian representative Holly Ferling, who received her new Carlton Brunswick playing uniform (still in its clear plastic wrapper), just as the umpires were walking out onto the field to start play.

She then emerged from the pavilion, in what seemed seconds, willing and ready to bowl the first over of the game.

Just as well it was the right size.

The match itself was a notable one, as South African international Mignon Du Preez (playing for Dandenong), smashed a Premier Cricket record T20 score of 142 from just 69 deliveries. It was an innings that included 13 fours and 7 sixes, many of which endangered several cars that were parked just beyond the square leg and mid wicket boundary, on one side of the ground.

De Preez wasn't particularly tall or powerful, but once she got her eye in, she smashed the bowling to all parts.

Determined to target the road side boundary, she would often step way across her stumps, exposing all three, as she aimed to loft the ball into the trees that were pretty much the only protection a row of parked cars had.

It was actually quite kind of her to target that particular side of the ground, as there was creek running alongside the opposite boundary, and I hate to think how many balls we might have lost if fielders were constantly searching for them 'in the drink.'

I had umpired Carlton Brunswick in a game the previous year and I must confess to feeling quite hurt that same day when one of their number, recognised me but couldn't remember my name.

'I'm sorry' she said, 'It's just slipped my mind.'

'Really?' I replied. 'You tried to kill me last year.'

Thankfully that remark seemed to spark some degree of recognition and memory of Carlton Brunswick's away fixture at Ringwood, when a howling gale was blowing directly across the ground.

The player in question was a talented and athletic left hander, who executed a powerful cut shot, that had I not managed to deflect with my hand (while still holding a plastic, if now broken ball counter), may well have taken my head clean off.

The ball seemed to arrive in the blink of an eye and the force of the blow knocked me to the ground.

At the time, I tried to quickly regain my feet and pretend that it was all really nothing, when in the process, I managed to fall over again, soliciting considerable concern from the players, to say nothing of re-enforcing my own embarrassment.

# CHAPTER THIRTY THREE
## DANDENONG

When I first joined the Premier Cricket umpires' panel, Dandenong was already a long established and successful stand alone women's club, that had won a very exciting 1st XI Grand Final the previous season, defeating long time rivals Box Hill in the process.

I went to watch the game, having only arrived back in the country a few weeks before, and I can remember being impressed no end with the skill and talent on display.

For one thing, I saw a Dandenong player (who has since embarked on a career in the AFLW), take the best outfield catch I have ever seen.

Dandenong were the Lions at this stage and they played their home games at Greaves Reserve, within the confines of the local showgrounds.

Their pavilion was spacious but little more than a single room, designed I dare say, to accommodate a football team.

Opposing teams would gather at either end of the space, while umpires (having stepped over various kit bags and stray pieces of equipment in the process), would get changed in the toilets that were accessed by a door in the far corner of the room.

I was never comfortable traversing a women's dressing room at the best of times, and I was very pleased to see the situation at Dandenong improve significantly, in a relatively short space of time.

A couple of years later, the pavilion at Greaves Reserve had been completely redeveloped. It now features individual dressing rooms for both teams, together with a kitchen, toilets and an area where everyone can gather for tea.

The umpires' room is accommodated at the rear of the building, and the door unlocked by means of a digital 'key card' - rather like an upmarket hotel.

I am not sure if it was an adherence to a local building regulation, or the fact that the architect had a rather twisted sense of humour, but it was hard not to be mildly offended to see (and feel), that the sign for the umpires' room was also written in Braille.

One of the first games I umpired at Greaves Reserve was a 2nd XI fixture against Brunswick Park.

Dandenong was in the field when one of the

Brunswick Park batters turned and hurried off in search of a second run, tearing a hamstring in the process.

To her great credit she bravely hobbled on and stumbled forward, trying to make good her ground before clutching at the back of her leg and collapsing on the pitch in a flood of tears.

A great hive of activity followed, as a succession of team mates and coaches ran onto the field to help, and it was some time before she was on her feet and assisted across the boundary.

As the drama was unfolding, a young Dandenong player sat cross legged by the side of the pitch, and once everything had settled down, she looked up at me rather quizzically and naively, asking 'Is that the end of the game?'

'Oh no' I said. 'She's just injured. She's not dead.'

The initial 1st XI fixture that I umpired at Greaves Reserve featured one of the greats of the women's game, in Dandenong's Sarah Elliott.

I had been listening to the Women's Ashes from England on the ABC until the early hours a few months before, and when I spoke to her after the game, I thanked her for remaining 95 not out overnight (at one point), in the only Test Match of the series.

As I explained, it was a circumstance that gave those of us listening to the game in Australia, the opportunity to hear her get a hundred, the following day at a reasonable hour.

It wasn't until a couple of years later, that I learned she had actually been up most the night, caring for her new born son, before securing the few runs she needed to get the job done later in the day.

There was no mistaking Sarah Elliott's ability as a cricketer. She batted with balance, poise and wonderful timing, while her bowling demonstrated great skill and guile.

I felt quite nervous introducing myself after that first match, and tremendously relieved when she proved to be every bit as warm and gracious, as she was talented.

A few weeks later, she was playing in another Dandenong 1st XI match, that I was appointed to umpire.

Our paths crossed before the game, once her team's warm up process had concluded, whereupon she recognised me, said hello and remembered my name.

It made my day.

Dandenong's Emma Gallagher had won 'Most Improved,' in my post season awards the previous year, and she provided a memorable moment of light relief in another home game the following season.

I remembered how she had managed to dismiss Meg Lanning, in the Grand Final two or three seasons before, and she was bowling her accurate and precise seamers from my end.

The first ball of her over, the striker played at and missed, and she did so again the very next ball. From her third delivery the striker managed to get a faint inside edge that saved her from a certain leg before wicket dismissal. The fourth ball she edged just beyond the reach of the wicket keeper, only to see it fall agonisingly short of a fielder at first slip, and from the fifth, she secured an inside edge that missed her leg stump by the proverbial cigarette paper, before crossing the boundary for four runs.

I don't think I have ever seen anyone more denied the slightest ounce of luck, in a single over on any cricket field, anywhere in the world, and as Gallagher turned around and walked back to her mark, she was quite justifiably muttering something entirely appropriate, and probably quite vulgar under her breath.

At this point I decided to take a risk, having witnessed a sequence of events so entirely devoid of good fortune, that it defied any semblance of logic.

As she walked past me, preparing to run in and deliver the final ball of the over, I turned towards her and said 'It's a stupid game isn't it.'

I quickly listed in my mind a series of probable outcomes;

1. She would simply ignore it and walk away, saying something quite rude and offensive about me as she did.
2. She would rebuke my remark with a derisory one of her own, such as 'Whatever.'
3. She would kick me in the shin.
4. All of the above.

To my great relief, surprise and unbridled delight however, she actually chose to exercise an option that I hadn't even considered.

She burst out laughing.

I think that moment said a lot about her, a lot about her club, her team mates and dare I say, a lot about women's cricket all over the world.

It is a just a game after all and every so often, a stupid one at that.

# Chapter Thirty Four
# A long way from Bairnsdale

Over the years, Dandenong has nurtured, developed and produced any number of outstanding players.

None more so than Sophie Molineux.

Having grown up in Bairnsdale (Eastern Victoria), Molineux played with a local club, alongside her father, often representing the Gippsland region in Cricket Victoria's underage pathway tournaments.

She is a very talented left arm, off spin bowler and clearly gifted with a bat in her hand, but it was an outstanding piece of fielding that first caught my eye one afternoon at Greaves Reserve.

She was fielding in the covers, when an opponent nudged a ball short of her position, before calling the non striker through for a run.

Molineux swooped on the ball and picked it up without breaking stride. She was balanced and poised in the blink of an eye, and hurled a powerful, flat and accurate throw that broke the stumps at the striker's end, before the wicket keeper had even arrived on the scene, leaving her opponent metres short of her ground.

It was one of those 'Wow moments,' when I had clearly witnessed something quite special, and seen a player of unrivalled potential.

The fact that Sarah Elliott 'anointed her' to me the very same day, was enough to erase any lingering doubt.

I remember announcing her to a group of people who were surrounding the scorers, immediately after the game, saying 'I tell you what, that Sophie Molineux can play.'

A woman (whom I suspect may well have been her mother), agreed enthusiastically, before I confirmed 'I would buy shares in her.'

Sophie Molineux did me a great favour a couple of years later, as I trudged away from the MCG in a shattered and desperate state, having seen my beloved Magpies fall just five points short of the West Coast Eagles in the 2018 AFL Grand Final.

It would have been an especially long and lonely drive home, save for the fact I was able to listen to Sophie and her Victorian team mate Georgia Wareham, making their debut for Australia in a one day international against New Zealand.

It was a wonderful antidote.

She was always destined to play at the highest level, but happily her schedule allowed her to turn out for Dandenong a few times during the season, whereupon she was as friendly, polite and respectful as ever.

She even chose to withdraw a rather ambitious LBW appeal when bowling one day, having realised that the ball she had delivered, would have otherwise missed the stumps.

'No, no I withdraw that' she said. 'I'm sorry. That's just embarrassing.'

'There's no need to apologise' I said, adding 'I've seen worse.'

'Really?' she wondered.

'Well, not many' I said.

# CHAPTER THIRTY FIVE
## ALARMING

The following season, the Dandy Lions became the Dandenong Panthers when they merged with an established men's Premier Cricket club and arranged to play the bulk of their 1st XI games on Sundays, at the club's headquarters - Shepley Oval.

I arrived to umpire my first Dandenong match of the season and finding the door to the umpires' room locked, went in search of someone who might have a key.

I climbed the stairs to the first floor of the grandstand and wandered into the kitchen, where I found someone who was associated with the club.

I explained the situation, and was soon after presented with a key.

I returned downstairs, walked across to the umpires' room, unlocked the door and carried my bag and hat inside.

No sooner had I put my bag down on a bench, than I could hear a sequence of high pitched beeps that appeared to be emanating from an alarm console in the far corner of room.

As if I didn't realise what was about to happen, the red flashing light above the key pad was a dead giveaway, as a loud, violent and ear splitting siren soon rung out.

I am not sure if it was intended to alert the police, the neighbours or simply to render any intruder clinically deaf, but it was as painful as it was embarrassing.

I walked outside and shouted to a couple of groundsmen, who were busily preparing the pitch, asking if they knew the numeric code that might shut the alarm off, but they just shrugged their shoulders and carried on.

I had no choice other than to return to the scene of the crime, and wait for a club official or the police to arrive.

Fortunately, an official won the race and I made a point of saving the relevant four digit code in the contact menu of my phone, just as soon as I could hear myself think.

The following season, the Dandenong 1st XI was

scheduled to play Ringwood on the adjoining Wilson Oval and I arrived at the ground to see a fellow standing amongst the Dandenong players, while resting what appeared to be a television camera on his shoulder.

It looked as though he was filming the team during their warm up and thinking it was probably all just part of a training exercise, I really didn't pay it much heed, as my colleague and I continued to set up the stumps and inspect the ground.

A few minutes later, we had called the captains over and were about to execute the toss, when the same bloke suddenly appeared, with the same camera perched on his shoulder, saying 'Don't worry about me. Just pretend I'm not here.'

Before I could say 'Who the hell are you anyway?' another fellow arrived on the scene, as if out of nowhere, and addressed both my colleague and me.

'G'day fellas' he said. 'Neil Kearney, Channel Seven.'

Apparently Kearney and his cameraman had been commissioned to produce a short story featuring Dandenong's Maryam Omar, who when not playing with her club or studying for a Master's Degree, could be seen playing with, and I believe captaining the

Kuwaiti women's cricket team.

Pleased as I was for Maryam, that she was about to command some well deserved attention, I thought it might have been nice if we had been given some advance notice of Channel Seven's presence and intentions, particularly as their cameraman was in the habit of running out into the middle of the ground during the game, to install and occasionally adjust a miniature camera behind the stumps.

It was far from ideal, and to her credit, the Ringwood captain was co-operative throughout, without being particularly impressed.

Above all though, if I did happen to sneak into shot in the background, just remember that the camera adds five kilos.

# CHAPTER THIRTY SIX
# ESSENDON MARIBYRNONG PARK

EMPLCC or Essendon Maribyrnong Park Ladies Cricket Club can rightfully boast the title of 'The oldest women's cricket club in the world,' having formed in 1905.

The club plays its home games at Aberfeldie Park, alongside the banks of Melbourne's Maribyrnong River, and it has to date, numbered several Australian players among its ranks.

In recent years this roster has included Kristen Beams, Molly Strano, Georgia Wareham and Elyse Villani (once of Brunswick Park/Prahran), while television commentator Melanie Jones had graduated not long before.

I was appointed to umpire several games at EMP in my first few seasons, which only serves to illustrate how little Cricket Victoria factors geography and travel considerations, into its umpiring appointments.

Aberfeldie Park was well and truly across town, but always a pleasure to visit and I managed to foster a good relationship with the club and make any number of friends in the process.

I was even given the nick name 'Duck' after a year or so, having been given every assurance that it related to the disparity between my own height and that of the entrance to the pavilion, but I was never totally convinced.

When I first came on board, the EMP pavilion resembled Dandenong's at Greaves Reserve, in as much as it was essentially a single space, that would accommodate both teams.

The most significant differences were that it was about half the size, and the umpires weren't accommodated in a toilet, so much as a store room.

All of the same hazards existed as at Dandenong. A point that was colourfully illustrated before one 2nd XI match when an EMP player stopped me in my tracks, just as I was beating a path to the umpires'/store room.

She explained that there was a kit bag lying in my way on the floor, which together with the fact that I was practically blind, might present a trip hazard, and that she wanted me to be careful, lest I fall over and hurt myself.

It was all very good natured and I played along, even seeking out her captain, suggesting she might want to speak to the player concerned, about her 'very rude and inappropriate behaviour.'

The captain indicated that she didn't think there was much she could do about it, then acting unhappy and frustrated with the situation, I made tracks to the room in question, managing to trip over the very same bag that I had been warned about just moments before.

Anyone would think the whole exercise had been carefully scripted, and I felt a complete fool, as great peals of laughter rang out.

A few years later the original EMP pavilion was demolished and replaced with a spacious, modern construction that resembled an aircraft carrier as much as a clubroom.

I suspect the architect was briefed to include an umpire's room in the new design. Note the emphasis on the singular, as what we were presented with was arguably comfortable enough for a single football referee to get showered and changed, but it was never going to work very well for two people simultaneously.

Mind you, the fact we could take a lift to and from the ground floor, was some measure of compensation.

A unique challenge that the club continues to face, is the preparation of a pitch each weekend during the season, and the ongoing maintenance of the outfield.

Aberfeldie Park is effectively a flood plain for the nearby river, and as a consequence, its soil contains a very high saline content, which doesn't agree too well with most species of grass.

At times the outfield was well below par, which has occasionally lead to matches being transferred to more suitable venues, and a couple of times we have played on pitches that I later described as 'diabolical' on the match report.

I remember one match that EMP played against Melbourne, when a bowler's delivery reared sharply and unexpectedly from a good length, hitting an EMP striker on the helmet, before deflecting towards fine leg.

The two batters completed one run, expecting a call of 'leg bye,' before I disallowed the run, as the striker had made no attempt to hit the ball with her bat, nor had she taken any clear evasive action.

Suffice to say the striker disagreed and made her feelings quite clear, asking me if I really thought that she 'wanted the ball to hit her in the head?'

By the strict 'Letter of the law,' one could probably

argue that it was the correct call, but having mulled it over in my mind at square leg for much of the next over, I decided to speak to her and her batting partner, before the next one commenced.

I asked the non striker if I could borrow her partner for a moment, then addressed the girl in question by name. I said that she was 'absolutely right, and that I had made a mistake.' I extended my hand, shook hers and said 'I apologise.'

Judging by the look on her face, it may well have been the first time anything like that had ever happened.

# CHAPTER THIRTY SEVEN
# HOT AND BOTHERED

Cricket is of course a summer sport and as a consequence it is occasionally played on very hot days.

Sadly, with global temperatures increasing year on year, that situation is likely to continue for some time yet.

The game of course originated in England, where temperatures above 30 degrees Celsius are considered extreme, and no one would have thought to factor the climatic conditions 'prevailing in the colonies,' into an eighteenth century equation, when the laws were being drafted.

I was appointed to umpire a match at Aberfeldie Park between EMP and Dandenong one day, when the temperature was forecast to reach at least 42 degrees.

My route to the ground took me past Flemington Racecourse where the Victorian Racing Industry had taken the entirely wise, responsible, and sensible action of cancelling all of the state's race meetings for that day.

Racing Victoria demonstrated enough sense not to expose horses, jockeys, trainers and spectators to such extreme conditions and having arrived at Aberfeldie Park, it was clear that the local men's cricket competition (one that was normally played on a neighbouring ground), had decided to cancel their own fixtures as well.

Cricket Victoria's 'Heat Policy' leaves the decision, as to whether play should start, stop or recommence on days with extreme temperatures, entirely to its umpires, and it educates them with a check list of 'symptoms' that players may present with, if they are adversely affected by extreme heat.

There is no consideration whatsoever given to umpires, only players.

Very few members of the Cricket Victoria premier umpires' panel have any medical qualification, and I can't imagine many of them (if any), would be capable of correctly assessing and acting in any such circumstance, when they themselves are just as likely to be adversely affected.

So it was for me, when I suffered 'Heat Stroke' in the second innings of the EMP v Dandenong match.

Curiously, I had been refusing to accept any drinks for several minutes, as I was convinced that I had already drunk too much, and that a vast reserve of fluid was sitting at the very top of my throat.

Apparently, this is a trick one's mind plays when it is seriously affected by extreme heat, and a definite sign that trouble is brewing.

Other than that, my own recollections are quite vague but I do recall feeling dizzy and disorientated while making my way off the ground.

I lost consciousness soon after, before 'coming to,' as my blood pressure was being taken.

At the time, I recall thinking that someone was gripping me very firmly by the arm and perhaps escorting me out of a night club, but once I managed to make sense of the paramedic's uniform and the fact that there was an ambulance parked a few feet away, I was able to piece things together.

One of the paramedics asked me my name, my age and what day it was.

I am pretty sure that I got the first two correct and happily I managed to suppress the urge to say 'Caulfield Cup Day' (for whatever reason), in response to the third. An answer that I dare say would have seen me loaded into the back of the attending ambulance and transported to the nearest hospital, given it was mid February.

I fought tooth and nail not to be taken to hospital, insisting that I was absolutely fine and that there was nothing whatsoever to worry about.

All of which was completely untrue.

My colleague continued to umpire on his own until the match concluded, before I suggested that he enter all of the relevant details into the match report, as I had absolutely no recollection of what had transpired during the game and still don't.

By this stage, a few hours had past and I had consumed a couple of energy drinks, to say nothing of the fact that I had been meticulously and very kindly cared for, by any number of players and club officials.

Feeling better and having insisted repeatedly that I was perfectly capable of driving home, I dragged my bag across the field to where my car was parked. I loaded everything I had with me into the boot, opened the driver's side door and soon after drove about 400 metres, as far as the local rowing club, where feeling horribly ill, I stopped the car, got out and sat by the river for the next two hours.

Thereafter I drove home in relatively short stints, stopping where I could to sit outside and relax for thirty or forty minutes at a time.

I completed my journey well after midnight and spent the rest of the day lying in bed, consuming nothing but water.

Since my Heat Stroke episode, I have refused to umpire cricket matches where the temperature is forecast to reach or exceed 40 degrees, and I am absolutely staggered that there has been no discernible change to Cricket Victoria's own Heat Policy.

I think there is a good chance a Victorian Premier Cricket umpire will be killed as a consequence of Heat Stroke one day.

Perhaps they will do something about it then.

# CHAPTER THIRTY EIGHT
## MELBOURNE

Melbourne Cricket Club made a long overdue entry into the Women's Premier Cricket competition, shortly before I returned from the UK.

Melbourne is of course a long established men's club, with generations of history, while it has always possessed facilities and resources that remain the envy of many.

Why it took the club as long as it did to introduce a women's cricket programme remains a mystery, but to be fair, having finally done so, it has achieved some tremendous results in a very short space of time.

Ambitiously, Melbourne entered teams in both the Women's Premier 1st and 2nd XI competitions from the outset, preferring to build and develop their talent pool, by recruiting players from local leagues across the state, rather than by poaching them from rival clubs.

As a consequence, results didn't come immediately. In their inaugural 2012/13 season, the Melbourne 1st XI won just one game, including a record breaking defeat to Box Hill, while their 2nd XI won just two.

Just six years later however, the club achieved the rare distinction of winning both the 1st and 2nd XI Women's Premierships, while the 2nd XI had also won the Premiership the previous season.

Melbourne is certainly an attractive option for any cricketer, male or female. The club plays most of its home games at the Albert Ground in St. Kilda Road, and failing that at an impressively re-developed facility in Beaumaris.

'The Albert,' actually rivals some of the best grounds where I umpired in the Kent League. It has always struck me as a blend of the St. Lawrence ground in Canterbury, and the Nevill ground in Tunbridge Wells.

It boasts an historic and attractive pavilion, with an umpires' room that is too small, but an otherwise spacious interior, kitchen and upstairs viewing balcony.

The ground itself is fenced and bordered by sloping banks of grass, all set beneath large, shady trees.

A number of timber benches, with metal frames, reclaimed from the top floor of the original MCG pavilion, are dotted around its perimeter.

It is a wonderful viewing ground, and a delightful place to umpire. The pitch is always immaculate, the players are talented, committed and friendly, while the outfield is invariably presented in magnificent condition.

Anyone would be happy for their daughter to play here.

I was appointed to a 2nd XI game between Melbourne and Plenty Valley at the Albert Ground one February when the temperature was forecast to reach and possibly exceed 38 degrees.

It marked the anniversary, more or less of my heat stroke episode at EMP, and I was very conscious of the fact that both teams included several girls that were marked as under fifteen years of age, on the team sheets that my umpiring colleague and I had collected from both captains at the toss.

Over the course of the next few minutes, I managed to convince my colleague that we should reduce the specified duration of the game from 45 overs to 35, so as to hopefully avoid any issues with the heat and player welfare.

We spoke with both the captains and communicated our decision.

Suffice it to say, it didn't go down well.

The captains and players were disappointed and unhappy, but it was the Melbourne team manager who picked up the proverbial gauntlet and ran a considerable distance with it.

In short, she gave me a furious and colourful lecture, telling me in no uncertain terms that cricket was a summer sport, while insisting that I had no right whatsoever to amend the format and duration of the game.

I decided that I would rather endure her vigorous protest, than deal with an angry parent whose child was being transported to the nearby Alfred Hospital in the back of ambulance.

Mind you, the way she carried on, I'm not entirely sure that wouldn't have been a better option.

The records will show that Melbourne bowled first and dismissed Plenty Valley for 85 runs in 26.1 overs.

They will also show, that Melbourne subsequently managed to pass Plenty Valley's total for the loss of three wickets in just 19.1 overs.

If only I had known.

# CHAPTER THIRTY NINE
## PLENTY VALLEY

Rather like Box Hill, Plenty Valley is not a stand alone women's club, nor is it affiliated with a men's Premier Cricket club. Both in fact, are associated with clubs whose men's teams play in Victoria's Sub District competition.

Plenty Valley is without doubt, the most far flung of all the women's clubs in the Premier Cricket competition. At least it is now that Napoleon Sebastapol, a team based in Ballarat that played in the 2nd XI competition, is no longer involved. Amen to that.

If EMP is 'across town,' then Plenty Valley is almost across the state - for me anyway.

Plenty Valley play some of their home games at the A K Line Reserve, which is in Watsonia, and most of them at Yarrambat War Memorial Park, which is in the middle of nowhere.

Games at Yarrambat are a great endorsement of satellite navigation, although to be fair, journeys there are without doubt the most scenic and attractive, in the entire competition.

The drive to Yarrambat takes me through areas like Greensborough, Eltham and Diamond Creek, regions that boast an abundance of gum trees and wildlife. It is almost like going on holiday.

Plenty Valley certainly presents a viable option for talented and committed female cricketers that happen to live north east of Melbourne, and one of its most notable graduates in recent years has been Tayla Vlaeminck, who having battled with any number of injuries early in her career, made her debut for Australia in a Test Match against England in 2019.

I first saw Vlaeminck open the bowling for Plenty Valley in a 1st XI match against Box Hill, a couple of years before.

She bowled the first over of the game, while I was standing at square leg, and I can remember thinking to myself, 'What is the wicket keeper doing all the way back there?'

Vlaeminck ran in and delivered the ball, which thudded into the keeper's gloves, before the striker's bat, while making a genuine attempt to play a shot I might add, had reached anything remotely resembling 'the perpendicular.'

If that first delivery didn't catch the striker's attention (which I very much doubt), it sure as hell woke me up, as in my experience there are very few bowlers in women's cricket who can bowl genuinely fast. Make no mistake, Tayla Vlaeminck is one of them and I just hope that her body can hold itself together for the duration of her cricketing career, as she is clearly a tremendous talent.

I believe she is studying physiotherapy at university. It may prove to be a wise career choice.

Other notable graduates of Plenty Valley have included former Victorian left arm all rounder Kirsty Lamb, who not unlike a number of others in the competition, was sadly lost to cricket when the lure of football and the AFLW presented itself.

Lamb achieved the rare distinction (by me at least), of being dubbed the David Rhys-Jones of women's football, when she managed to get herself reported in her very first AFLW game, but sadly that setback hasn't seen her return to the cricketing ranks.

# CHAPTER FORTY
## PRAHRAN

Prahran is a long established men's Premier Cricket club that saved itself a lot of time and effort, when inducting two women's teams into its own ranks, simply by absorbing the entire Brunswick Park structure, after it had spent the previous season playing as Brunswick.

Notwithstanding the expense involved in acquiring three different playing uniforms, in the space of three years, the transition seemed as seamless as it was successful, given Prahran managed to enlist Australian players Nicole Bolton and Jess Duffin (nee Cameron) in the process.

Duffin announced her arrival at Toorak Park in a match against Dandenong, hitting a ball for six that sent the scorers ducking for cover, as it smashed through a window of their elevated viewing box, at the top of the grandstand.

My own 'memorable moment,' at Toorak Park

was arguably less spectacular.

I was appointed to umpire a 1st XI fixture between Prahran and Box Hill - a game that featured no shortage of Victorian and Australian players.

Prahran batted first and accumulated 286 runs from their allocated 50 overs, with Elyse Villani joining the '98 Club,' when she nicked an otherwise innocuous and harmless leg side delivery to the wicket keeper.

My own contribution came immediately after tea, with Nicola Hancock bowling the opening over from the southern end of the ground, to (at that stage), future Australian captain Meg Lanning.

Hancock ran in and sent down a fast, accurate delivery that reared sharply from just short of a length. Lanning played at it and a split second later the ball was resting in the wicket keeper's gloves.

The bowler generated a boisterous and enthusiastic appeal for caught behind, as did the keeper herself, and all of the fielders in the vicinity.

I hadn't heard, or seen anything that gave me any reason to suspect that the striker had hit the ball, so I shook my head from side to side and said 'Not out.'

I don't blame Prahran for being unhappy. After all Box Hill had not registered a single run on the score board at this stage, and without Meg Lanning at the crease, it was hard to see them getting anywhere near the runs required.

The disappointment and frustration among the Prahran contingent was obvious, as I turned to the non striker and said 'I appear to have lost a few friends.'

To the Prahran players credit however, they soon put the incident behind them and we got on with what proved to be a tremendous game.

A few hours later, Box Hill managed to secure what had at times, seemed an unlikely victory in what was a very close and exciting finish.

With just two balls to spare they scored the winning runs, with Meg Lanning still at the crease having made 177 not out.

So it's not like it mattered.

# CHAPTER FORTY ONE
## RIGHETTI OVAL

Prahran's 2nd XI play most of their games at the Righetti Oval in Kooyong, a ground that is hidden away, nestled between Gardiner's Creek, the Monash Freeway and the Glen Waverley Line.

On Sundays, the park is heavily populated with dogs, that at times seem to outnumber humans.

There is a water tap that is set in the ground, in front of the pavilion. It features a single faucet, suspended from a pipe that is attached to a timber post. The tap itself, sits about two and half feet above the ground, and it is no doubt there primarily, for the benefit of dogs and their owners.

There is no drain beneath it, and no metal grate set above a pipe at its base. Excess water from the tap, simply accumulates on the ground, where the local dogs seem quite happy to lap up a few mouthfuls and move on.

Well, most dogs anyway.

I had arrived at Righetti Oval to umpire a match between Prahran and EMP. My colleague and I had just executed the toss with the captains and were walking off the field, when we caught sight of a full grown blond Labrador, charging full tilt towards the puddle of water that that had accumulated beneath the tap.

I thought the dog must be awfully thirsty, before he literally leapt towards the water, from a distance of at least two metres, twisting his ample and sturdy frame in mid air, so that he landed on his side, absolutely flush with the puddle itself. He managed to splash anyone, or anything that happened to be in the vicinity, then writhed and rolled in the mud for several seconds, getting as filthy as possible. He then stood up, looking very pleased with himself, before rushing back to his owners, and an appointment with the garden hose.

## Chapter Forty Two
## A Big Finish

One day the Prahran 2nd XI was scheduled to play its last match of the season at Toorak Park. It was an event that clearly coincided, with a post season function for most, if not all, of the club's men's teams, who had gathered in an entertainment room, next to the scorer's box at the top of the grandstand.

As the day wore on and as more and more beer seemed to have been consumed, I was starting to worry that some of the support and barracking that was emanating from the room, might prove to be less tasteful and appropriate than it might otherwise have been.

Happily that didn't prove to be the case at all and the Prahran girls in particular, seemed to enjoy the extra attention.

I even managed to milk the crowd myself at one point, when the home team was batting in the second innings of the match.

I was standing at the bowler's end, when the striker hoisted a ball high over mid wicket to the far side of the ground.

The ball landed a considerable distance from the 'crowd,' and many of them were clearly excited at the prospect that it may in fact have cleared the boundary rope, with several shouting 'How big is it?!' 'How big is it?!'

I confirmed the outcome of the shot with my colleague, then turned to the scorers, who were located immediately adjacent to the anxious spectators. I paused for a moment or two then signalled 'six,' soliciting a tremendous roar from those gathered at the top of the grandstand.

Soon after, the same girl who had hit the six, managed to score the winning runs, whereupon she strode from the field, raising her bat to acknowledge the cheers and applause of an adoring crowd.

Well done Prahran C.C.

# CHAPTER FORTY THREE
# RINGWOOD

Ringwood's ascension within the Premier Cricket competition came about quite slowly.

For several years, the Ringwood 1st XI played in the Premier 2nd XI competition, while the club's 2nd XI played in the top level of the Women's Community Cricket competition and so on.

It wasn't until the 2018/19 season, when Women's Premier Cricket was finally structured to include eight 1st XI teams and eight 2nd XI teams, all representing the same clubs, that Ringwood advanced to the top level.

Entering the 1st XI competition was always going to be a challenge, as despite the demands of the WBBL (together with various state and national commitments), Victoria's representative players often found time to turn out for their club sides.

For the most part though, and to Ringwood's great

credit, they stuck to the task, and concentrated on developing their own pool of talent.

I had a discussion about this very point with the club's 1st XI scorer, team manager and general father figure in Peter Kaspar, when I was appointed to a Ringwood game at Dandenong.

We were chatting before the match and I was telling him how thrilled I was to learn that Ringwood's own emerging talent, Tess Flintoff, was now a member of the Melbourne Stars outfit that had played in the WBBL competition during the week.

Peter was very proud of the fact that she, and other young girls playing Premier Cricket, had come so far at such a young age, and that they were very much a product of the commitment and hard work that people like him, and other club volunteers had devoted.

It was clear that he was absolutely thrilled for her, and he became quite emotional, as he was telling me so.

I for one was quite grateful that he did. For a while there, I thought it was just me.

Ringwood turned out that day with a new player, and a new captain in Bhavi Devchand.

Devchand had a been a member of the Perth

Scorchers squad in the WBBL, and though I am not entirely sure how or why she crossed the entire country to end up at Ringwood, it became clear over the course of the afternoon, that her club had secured the services of someone with a 'cricket brain.'

Ringwood won the toss, chose to bat and Devchand made a duck, but she still managed to play an important and crucial role in Ringwood's victory, once her team took the field.

The manner in which she rotated her bowlers worked very well, but it was the field placements she set, together with the respect and attention that her team afforded her that made all the difference.

Ringwood was defending a modest total of 128. A score that Dandenong, with 50 overs at its disposal, could be expected to chase down.

From the outset however, runs were difficult to come by, and boundaries particularly rare, as Devchand, working with what she had and recognising the task at hand, managed to turn the screw, and apply 'score board pressure' throughout the Dandenong innings.

She always seemed to be ahead of the game, anticipating what was about to happen, and having a plan in place before it did.

Wickets fell steadily, some to good bowling and catching, but others to the fact that the flow of runs was gradually being choked off, and as a consequence, Dandenong's task became more and more difficult.

Eventually, Dandenong was bowled out for 114 in the 33rd over.

I hope Bhavi Devchand stays with Ringwood for a while yet. She might be just what they need.

# CHAPTER FORTY FOUR
## ALCHEMY

Turf cricket pitches have long fascinated me.

Their preparation and development is a dark art, undertaken pre-season and during the week by horticultural alchemists, who manage to magically transform an otherwise bland strip of grass, into a clearly defined and viable playing surface.

Given umpires generally arrive an hour or so before the start of a match, we only ever get to see the finished product, and the fact remains, all I really know about turf pitches, is that three stumps should be set up at each end.

What I can say, without fear of contradiction, is that no two cricket pitches are ever the same. Each one is a unique reflection and representation of its local environment, as much as the many hours that had been meticulously devoted to its creation.

I always find it quite amusing, to see groups of

players surrounding a pitch before the start of a game. They will study it intently and discuss it thoroughly, often kneeling down to press their fingers against its surface, without ever having the faintest idea of just how it will behave throughout the course of the afternoon.

Some of the pitches where Shipbourne played its Sunday friendlies were practically under water. So damp and sodden that no one dare press their fingers into the surface, for fear they might lose a wrist watch.

During my tenure as captain, I was always reluctant to bat first in any such circumstance, worried that new ball bowlers, in particular, might inflict a nasty injury, with a delivery that would pitch just short of a length, only to rear sharply, menacing a batsman's ear, as it travelled towards the wicket keeper.

Occasionally that did indeed prove to be the case but more often than not, such offerings would stick in the surface of the pitch, emerging so slowly that the striker had time to shake off his gloves and kneel down to tie a shoelace, before the ball actually arrived.

The laws of the game stipulate that the pitch remain the responsibility of the curator until the captains have tossed. Only then is it handed over to the umpires. I think that is only fair, given the tremendous amount of work that so many groundsmen and women undertake during the week, and on match day mornings. All of which is enacted, before they have occasion to mark out the creases and finish rolling.

Curators are a curious breed, and I feel sure there are some among them who would prefer no one ever encroach, let alone play, on their creations at all.

Even so, they are unsung heroes, one and all.

# CHAPTER FORTY FIVE
# YOUTH PREMIER LEAGUE

Arguably, the best initiative that Cricket Victoria has implemented in recent years, has been what it now calls its Youth Premier League.

Even in the short time that I have been involved, it has been known as the Pathways Program and Victorian State Championships, without any discernible change in its structure.

The Youth Premier League is a state wide underage cricket competition, for both girls and boys.

It presents young cricketers with the opportunity to represent their respective metropolitan or country region, within a specified age group, and to play a series of games in a tournament format, during the school holidays, before a final (often), at the MCG.

The competition comprises eight teams from metropolitan regions and eight from the country, while these are in turn divided into two groups, each under the Renegades or Stars banner.

The boys' structure consists of teams in the Under 14, Under 16 and Under 18 age groups, while the girls' structure comprises teams aged Under 15 and Under 17.

Each region is specifically branded and allocated a distinctive name and logo, while players and coaches together, are presented with colourful training and playing uniforms.

It is all designed to create an impression of representation, where the Western Waves might set out to defeat the Inner East Emus, while the Gippsland Pride takes on the North West Wizards.

Consistent with my commitment to Women's Premier Cricket, I made myself available to umpire as many of the girls matches as I could, and notwithstanding the fact that each day entailed a rather dire mid week commute into Melbourne from the Mornington Peninsula, the entire exercise was a lot of fun.

Players clearly loved their uniforms and the fact that they were representing their own region, to say nothing of the opportunity to play with and against their friends, both old and new.

Teams from country regions also had the pleasure of staying at some of Melbourne University's residential colleges, for the duration of the competition.

Sadly, a few individuals were sent home early, when the odd curfew was ignored, but for the most part, everything seemed to run pretty smoothly.

Mind you, umpires only had to turn up on the day, and not keep squad members in check throughout the night.

I recognised quite a few players who were already playing with Premier Cricket teams, and it soon became clear which regions were affiliated with which clubs.

The concept was a great way to showcase the talent that the state possessed, and it has certainly proven a viable and worthwhile pathway, for any number of players in the past.

Over the course of just a few years, I think what struck me the most, was just how much the playing standard had improved.

There is no doubt that if talented, committed and athletic young girls are given access to the sort of coaching and training that they deserve, and happily are these days, the future of women's cricket in this country is very bright indeed.

When I recently umpired a series of Under 15 girls' matches, I remarked to a couple of coaches and officials afterwards, that the Under 15s of that year would have given their region's Under 17 squad a run for their money, just a year or two before, and each year, one or two player names would always make it onto my 'Watch List.'

One year, I managed to right somewhat of the wrong, that I believe I had been dealt at Mote Park in Maidstone some years before, when I was denied the opportunity to dismiss a batsman 'Hit the Ball Twice.'

I was standing at square leg in an Under 15 girl's game at Chelsworth Park in Ivanhoe.

We were playing on a synthetic pitch, and as the striker stepped back to defend a delivery, the ball bounced behind her feet, and then above her waist, threatening to hit the stumps.

Instinctively, she took one hand from her bat, and swatted the ball away, when a handful of fielders expressed their 'concern,' including a girl fielding just a few feet from me.

'She can't do that' she said.

I didn't dare turn to face her, and instead looked to one side, muttering from the corner of my mouth 'Appeal.'

'What?' she said.

'Appeal' I said a little louder.

'How's that?!' she called out, whereupon my colleague (standing at the bowler's end), apologised to the striker, and explained that he had no choice other than to give her out, while I was busy suggesting to the fielder in question, that we keep what had just transpired strictly between ourselves.

The striker strode from the field looking rather nonplussed, and as she walked passed me, I was able to explain what had happened, and why she had in fact contravened the relevant law.

Happily she didn't seem too concerned or upset.

Needless to say, I left out the bit about me prompting the fielder to appeal and if an angry coach or parent should subsequently protest, I decided that I would adopt the erstwhile famous 'Bart Simpson Defence.'

'I didn't do it. Nobody saw me do it. You can't prove a thing.'

# Chapter Forty Six
## Tedious and Dreary

All too often, I was disappointed with and occasionally angered, by the attitude that some of my male umpiring colleagues brought to Women's Premier Cricket matches.

All too frequently, on match days, I had barely said hello or introduced myself, before a colleague felt the need to explain why it was that he happened to be appointed to that day's game.

A common refrain was that the men's competition was in the midst of a two day game cycle (when a single match was played over consecutive weekends), and given the fellow I was umpiring with that day wasn't available the previous weekend or the next, he had effectively 'dropped out of sync' with the roster of appointments, and would otherwise be putting his feet up.

Other times, they just complained and whinged,

insisting they were above it all.

Given we would be spending the next few hours together, it's not something I bothered to challenge, nor is it something I understood.

The worst exchange I ever endured, came at a mid-season meeting, when I was extolling the virtues and talent of one player in particular, to a fellow umpire.

I explained how much that I thought this particular girl had improved, how dynamic and aggressive she was with the bat, and what a brilliant athletic fielder she had become, possessed of a powerful arm.

My colleague absorbed none of it. He simply stared at me, with a look that I can best describe as one of determined bewilderment.

'You know she's a lesbian?!' he said.

I fired back 'I don't want to marry her! I just think she's a good cricketer!'

I then turned my back, saying aloud, (I hope audibly) 'dickhead.'

If winter classes were a drag, then the T & D meetings we were expected to attend throughout the season were akin to torture.

Officially, T & D stands for 'Training and Development' but you need only glance at my own diary entries for the coinciding dates, to see that I continued to dub them 'Tedious and Dreary.'

Cricket Victoria umpires are expected to travel, three or four times a season, to the Junction Oval in St. Kilda, to attend a professional collective, that more often than not, is a meeting for the sake of having a meeting.

I can't recall a single instance where the information conveyed couldn't have been encompassed in an email, while some of the content presented was simply absurd.

By the time we had our third Umpiring Manager (during my tenure), we were still being told, time and again, just how professional we were expected to be and how important we all were, while at other times, we were asked to wander around the room in small groups, completing a personality profile, that would ultimately define which Simpsons character we most resembled.

At one stage, we were all placed into smaller, specialised groups and summoned to St. Kilda one evening, where we were asked to collectively discuss the concept of 'Elite Honesty.'

I have a zero tolerance for corporate clichés and buzz words at the best of times, and I had no intention whatsoever of making the slightest contribution to such a ridiculous and futile consideration.

Hall of Fame racehorse trainer Colin Hayes once said 'There are no degrees of honesty.' That's good enough for me.

To my mind, the nonsense of 'Elite Honesty,' was akin to an obstetrician telling a patient she was sort of pregnant.

# Chapter Forty Seven
# The Oft Forgotten

Some of the most important people involved with cricket clubs, certainly on match days, are scorers.

Not every club is lucky enough to have someone willing and able to volunteer their time each week, and to the best of my knowledge, no training courses for scorers even exist in Victoria.

Shipbourne C.C. was blessed to have a dedicated full time scorer in Andy 'Pebbles' Beach, who would dutifully show up to record every Saturday 1st XI match and every Sunday friendly.

'Pebbles' has meticulously recorded every delivery and every outcome, in all of Shipbourne's matches for several years, and I can say from personal experience, that he continues to exercise the highest degree of integrity, as he ignored and rejected every bribe and threat that I could throw at him, that fateful afternoon at Hurst Green.

I 'suggested' to him (more than once), after the game, that all he had to do was find just two runs, somewhere else in the score book, and re-allocate them to my personal batting total.

History would then record the 'fact,' that at long last, I had compiled my first and only three figure score, but to paraphrase former UK Prime Minister Margaret Thatcher - The scorer was not for turning.

The next time Cricket Victoria's umpires are invited to discuss the concept of 'Elite Honesty,' we should fly 'Pebbles' out from the UK.

It is always a great comfort to umpires, to know that they have dedicated and professional scorers to work with, even if those same people take a perverse delight in alerting anyone in the vicinity, to the fact that a five ball over had ensued at some point during the innings.

In the game's earliest days, scores were recorded by means of notches carved onto a stick, and for decades, hand written entries in a printed scorebook have more than sufficed, when it came to compiling and presenting a meticulous and detailed record of any match, at any level.

I can remember scoring games of backyard cricket, using the sheets printed in the rear section of that summer's ABC Cricket Book, while others did the same when listening to, or watching Test Matches of the era.

Sadly, cricket scoring is becoming more and more computerized, with laptops simultaneously updating score boards and web sites, allowing a community of fans anywhere in the world, to follow the progress of matches in real time, online.

I am sure any number of people would consider such things a wonderful innovation, but I think it is a shame in many respects, as cricket score books can be, and often are, works of art.

Winnie Warman was a scorer for many years in Kent, and her husband Roy was one of the tutors at the first umpires' training course that I attended in Sevenoaks.

Winnie presented a course in cricket scoring herself, and any scorebook that she had completed for the duration of a match, was a thing of beauty.

Not only did she have the neatest and most concise handwriting that I have ever seen, she showed up at each game, with a collection of ultra fine, felt tipped pens in a selection of colours.

The idea was that each bowler would be devoted a different colour, and that any runs a batsmen scored from any delivery that any particular bowler sent down, would also be recorded in that same colour, within his or her own personal total. Similarly any extras such as No balls, Wides, Byes, Leg byes and so on, would appear in that bowler's particular colour.

As a consequence, it was possible to pick up one of Winnie's score books at the end of a match, or years hence, and follow the progress of a game ball by ball, simply by tracking each bowler's individually defined colour.

Pages from some of her score books should be framed and hung on a wall, as even if no one should bother to chart the course of the matches they record, each one presents a unique and colourful template. A cricketing kaleidoscope if you will.

I have always been very grateful to the scorers, in any match that I have umpired, even if I have fallen foul of them on occasion.

I was given a pretty harsh lecture following the Women's 1st XI T20 final one year, when apparently, I hadn't signalled quickly enough to the scorers following each relevant delivery.

I tried to explain that regardless of the tempo that shorter format games might adopt, umpires could only signal to the scorers once the ball was 'dead.'

Suffice to say that didn't stand.

'You were so bloody slow!' I was told, to which I quite calmly replied;

'I think you will find the word is laconic.'

Nonetheless, I am always anxious to thank the scorers at the conclusion of any innings or match, which has sadly back fired, and stoked the fury of some more than once.

As players and umpires are leaving the field, the scorers are invariably adding up the bowling figures and requisite extras, before double checking each other's records of the same. The last thing they need is an umpire interrupting that process, offering his thanks and a handshake.

I have incurred a scorer's wrath any number of times and am clearly a slow learner, as however well intentioned, it continues to happen.

All the same, I am very pleased to see end of season club and team photos that include scorers. They most certainly deserve to be included, and it is only fitting they be recognised in such a manner.

While often hidden away for much of the match, the role of the scorers is every bit as important as that of the umpires, and anyone should be encouraged to acknowledge and appreciate their contribution.

Mind you, if you decide to do so yourself, it's probably best to wait a few minutes, once the game has finished.

## CHAPTER FORTY EIGHT
## HALLOWED TURF

Every so often, an interesting umpiring opportunity presented itself, and one such example surfaced when I answered a phone call from Mark Hanton.

'Are you available Wednesday next week?' he said, adding 'I want you to umpire a match at the MCG.'

'I am now' I replied.

The match he was talking about, was a corporate entertainment fixture for members of Cricket Victoria's 'Hassett Club.'

As far as I could tell, the 'Hassett Club' was a semi regular luncheon group. An opportunity for serious cricket fans to meet, eat and network a few times a year. It was all presented under the Cricket Victoria banner and I dare say the opportunity to play a game on the Melbourne Cricket Ground once a year, was a pretty juicy carrot, when it came to stumping up the annual membership fee.

I was probably about twelve years old when I last set foot on the playing surface of the MCG. That was back in the day when kids could have a kick of the footy on the ground itself, after what was then a VFL match.

A lot had changed since then. All of the grandstands and the Members' Pavilion had been demolished and rebuilt, while two huge video scoreboards (both of which were operating the day we were there), adorned each end of the ground.

To Cricket Victoria's credit, it did all it could to create a memorable 'Match Day Experience' for everyone involved. The teams and umpires were introduced over the public address system, with our names echoing from the vast empty grandstands, as a small crew of contractors, who effectively constituted the entire crowd, were busily renovating one of the corporate boxes in the Olympic Stand.

It was a great photo opportunity, and my colleague and I exchanged smart phones to that effect, when not enlisting one of the groundsmen to get a shot of us together.

We played one match in the morning, and another in the afternoon, with teams rather unimaginatively defined as Red, Blue and Green, according to the colour of the shirts they were wearing.

No sooner had the first match started, than it dawned on me that I had absolutely no idea where the scorers were located. In fact, after speaking to my colleague and taking a quick poll of all the participants on field at the time, it was clear that no one did.

As a consequence, I was able to absorb much of the scale and majesty, of the (albeit empty) grandstands, as I searched for any hint or indication, as to just where on earth they were.

In the end, I simply gave up and continued to signal to the scoreboard at the City End of the ground, even though there was never any acknowledgement that followed.

Several overs had been completed before I finally caught a glimpse of a flashing red light, shining from a window in the distance, next to the terrace level of the Members' Stand.

It was clearly the scorers trying to catch my attention, and I suspect the sequence of red flashes they were presenting me with, may well have been Morse Code for 'We're over here you idiot!'

I waved enthusiastically and gratefully, while trying to convey something of an apology from the best part of a hundred metres, before we got on with the game.

Both of the matches were played in a pleasant manner and in a good spirit, while Emma Inglis and Bob Quiney (members of the state's two representative teams), had been rostered on to wander amongst the fielders throughout, looking bored and disinterested.

At one point, a boisterous and confident appeal for caught behind erupted, when the bowler, wicket keeper and various members of the fielding side seemed convinced that a delivery had deflected from a batman's glove, as he tried to play a pull shot.

As their echoing cries died down, I dismissed the appeal, which needless to say, initiated the usual recriminations of disbelief and head shaking.

The bowler had just reached his mark, and was preparing to run in again, when I glanced up at the scoreboard to see that its operator had 'frozen' a key moment from the preceding delivery, in a video replay.

The image showed the batsman in the process of playing his shot, the ball literally resting atop his forearm, before it travelled through to the wicket keeper.

I extended my left arm and stepped across to block the bowler's path, before pointing at the scoreboard and directing everyone's attention to the image it displayed.

'Let's hang on a minute!' I called out, adding 'Now before we move on. Can we all see?!'

I may never get the chance to see a decision of mine so comprehensively verified again in the future, and I wasn't about to waste this one.

# CHAPTER FORTY NINE
## EXTRAS

Another additional appointment that I managed to secure, was umpiring the Melbourne Stars Women in a practice match at Melbourne Grammar School.

The Stars squad would play two T20 matches against the school's 1st XI on the main oval, where I would have to relive the shame and trauma of dropping a regulation catch decades before - an episode that arguably cost my team victory in the House Cricket Final.

The match preceded the first season of the WBBL competition and it was exciting to see some of the stars of the Premier Cricket competition in action, together with a couple of English imports, who clearly had the sense to escape a British winter, when the opportunity presented itself.

I imagine it was familiar territory for Meg Lanning, who had not only played in Carey Grammar's 1st XI while she was in her final year at school, but also in the Associated Public Schools representative team that same year.

Both games were played in a serious but friendly manner, while the Stars coach asked my colleague and me not to be too generous, when it came to judging and calling any wides that his bowlers might deliver.

At one point in the Stars innings, Dandenong captain Kelly Applebee drove a ball hard and straight over the bowler's head, towards the Domain Road end of the ground, where her teammates had gathered.

They were clearly all looking forward to applauding a six, when I suspect the ball landed just inches inside the boundary, such was the collective sigh of disappointment that followed.

I signalled a boundary four to the scorers, just as one player called out 'Give it to her anyway!'

Given there was really nothing much at stake, I shouted back 'You should have cheered. I would have bought it!'

At the end of the day, the game tally was one all, and both teams gathered and mingled together with teachers and coaches for a photo opportunity.

It reminded me of the aftermath of the Lashings games at Sevenoaks several years before, when my umpiring colleague Ian Fraser and I were invited to take part and included in the official post match photos. That's me standing next to Phil DeFreitas and Mohammed Akram, as evidenced by the framed photograph that hangs on the wall next my desk to this day.

As parents, siblings and friends all scrambled for position, no one thought to include the umpires. We just stood idly by and watched.

That was until one woman (I dare say a parent of one of the boys), approached me saying 'Mister Umpire, you're tall. Can you stand here and take a photo of everyone for me?'

She handed me a digital camera and I stood at the back of the parental throng, taking a couple of shots of 'everyone.'

Soon after, one of the teachers invited my colleague and me to enjoy some post match soft drinks and sandwiches with both teams.

I declined.

There was a much nicer post script to a couple of practice matches that I umpired between the Victorian Under 18 girls squad, and a boys team that was collectively a few years younger, and an underage representative team from the Gippsland region.

The matches were played at the Bundalaguah Cricket Club, somewhere between Sale and Maffra.

I drove to the venue, collecting my colleague on the way.

We had been told the Victorian girls were an Under 15 team, and I was surprised when soon after we arrived, that the first person to say hello was Sophie Molineux, who being from Gippsland herself, clearly didn't have to travel quite as far.

I asked if she was there in a coaching capacity, when she explained that she was the captain of the Under 18 girls, and that it was in fact the boys' team that was aged, more or less under 15 years of age.

This was a terrific and surprising bonus, given as much as I was looking forward to umpiring a group of talented youngsters, I would in fact be standing with a team of older girls, almost all of whom I knew quite well from their respective Premier Cricket clubs.

The only 'overage' girl, who was in fact there in a coaching capacity, was Australian representative Molly Strano - the reigning queen of the WBBL.

The weather was fine, the standards high and the day simply flew by, before we found ourselves in the umpires' room again, packing our bags and preparing to leave.

Moments later, there was a knock at the door, and one of the Cricket Victoria coaches poked his head inside, inviting my colleague and me into the team's dressing room 'for a moment.'

We arrived, just as the coach passed the baton to Georgia Wareham (one of the more senior players), who made a really lovely speech, saying how grateful that all of the girls were that we had travelled as far as we had, to help out and umpire the day's matches.

It was worth the time and effort for that alone.

# Chapter Fifty
## English History

Apparently, the original Lime tree that had been standing in the outfield of Kent's St. Lawrence Cricket Ground in Canterbury, had been diseased for several years, and given its demise was considered inevitable, the club had been growing a replacement at a nearby nursery for some time.

I have often thought what I might have done, for the fifteen or so years that followed, had that tree not met its end when it did.

Its demise seemed to coincide seamlessly with the cricket umpire training courses, that were being presented across the county.

From the course conveners' perspective, the idea had been to recruit students from the playing ranks and associates of Kent's various cricket clubs, while the opportunity to tack a paragraph onto the end of an article in the local paper, was little more than an opportune afterthought.

When I first signed up and handed over my £30, I never had any intention of actually umpiring. The course was just something to do in the winter and it was only after I completed the same endeavour, the following year, and sat a secondary level exam, that I decided I should actually give it a shot.

At the time, I think I saw it as an opportunity to further immerse myself into the culture of a country that was so steeped in history, as much as it was a chance to a earn a few quid on the weekends.

Whatever my initial motivation may have been, I soon discovered that I loved being a cricket umpire. I had the best seat in the house, and the best view of a wonderful and ancient game, in some of the most beautiful surroundings in the world.

I remember my very first game at Meopham like it was yesterday, aided by the fact a print of the cricket ground hangs on the wall to my left - one of many English cricket souvenirs that adorn the walls and bookshelves surrounding my desk.

I recall seeing an email from Sevenoaks Vine C.C. that was being widely circulated a few years ago. The club was cataloguing its history and the email's author was asking if anyone knew the whereabouts of an original oil painting of the cricket ground and pavilion, created some years before, by renowned local artist Graeme Lothian.

A print of the painting was hanging in the club's pavilion, but no one (including the artist), seemed to have any idea what had happened to the original.

It must have broken their hearts to learn 'That bloody Australian umpire bought it at an exhibition and took it home with him.'

The painting has hung over my desk for years and it always will. I look at it every single day. It is a magnificent image, and a constant and delightful reminder of a very special time and place.

The Salix cricket bat that Andrew Kember made for me leans against the bookshelf. It needs a new grip, but is otherwise in good condition, while the kit bag that houses my pads, gloves and Shipbourne playing attire, lives in the garage.

The bat features in two photographs that sit side by side above the bookshelf behind my desk. They were taken at a Shipbourne home game. I am not quite sure who the opposition is, but one shows me playing what looks like a half decent cover drive, and in the other, I am strolling casually between the wickets, looking quite relaxed and pleased with myself. Perhaps it went for four.

If only that straight drive at Hurst Green had.

# Chapter Fifty One
## Australian History

I never really had the opportunity to umpire any women's cricket in England, with the sole exception being a regional underage, indoor tournament that was held at Sevenoaks School.

Matches were played on adjoining basketball courts, while parents, friends and team mates watched and barracked from elevated viewing balconies.

The stature of the contest was grossly exaggerated, as any sound that anyone made, was amplified tenfold, as it bounced off the walls and ceiling. The arena became a deafening cauldron at times, and at one point, I was enlisted to stand in one of the balconies between two groups of parents, who had almost come to blows in a lead up game, when the same two teams met in a final.

Fortunately everyone behaved themselves, and 'security' (such as it was), wasn't called upon.

It must be said, the players themselves were a

delight to deal with throughout, regardless of the circumstances or outcome of any game. They seemed entirely oblivious to the cacophony that often surrounded them, and happy enough just to be out there, playing a game with their friends.

All the same, I reckon if I could cope with the atmosphere and distractions of that event, I could handle just about anything that was likely to develop on a cricket field.

I count myself tremendously lucky to have umpired Women's Premier Cricket in Victoria, and I am very grateful that Umpiring Manager Bob Parry granted my initial request, and that his successors have seen fit to retain the arrangement.

My return to Australia coincided with a veritable explosion of interest and investment in the women's game, and I have seen any number of talented female cricketers develop and advance to play for their state, their country and various WBBL franchises since.

I have been privy to some magnificent performances in the Women's 1st XI competition, and I have witnessed some great potential in the seconds, while a few words of encouragement or a simple compliment to a girl playing in the Under 15s, is often enough to see her face simply light up.

Any compliments I dispense are sincere and quite rare, including the one I paid Dandenong's Irish import Kim Garth, when she sent down a nigh on unplayable delivery, that squared up a Box Hill opponent, before crashing into her off stump.

'In this country, that's what we call an absolute ripper' I said.

Modestly, she replied 'I think she just missed a straight one.'

'Are you kidding?' I protested. 'That would have bowled just about anyone.'

She seemed quite grateful and pleased with my assessment, before I added 'Probably not me.'

Of course, the only reason I included that caveat, was the fact that she would have almost certainly dismissed me several overs beforehand and as a consequence, she wouldn't have had to waste such an outstanding delivery, on someone who would have missed it by about a foot.

I have enjoyed a great relationship with any number of players and captains over the years, while always striving to maintain a 'professional detachment.'

The simple fact is, I respect what the players do, I admire their ability, and I appreciate how they play the game.

As my friend Neil Kerrison reminded me, before my Kent League first division debut. 'It's just another game of cricket.'

Above all though, the atmosphere and environment that enshrines Women's Premier Cricket in Victoria, is the closest thing I have ever known to umpiring cricket in England, and that is indeed a rare and sincere compliment.

Female cricketers the world over have an inherent respect for the history and traditions of the game, while its spirit is ingrained in the contest throughout.

As unlikely and unplanned, as my cricket umpiring journey has been, I will always be grateful to my colleagues and mentors, to say nothing of the players, scorers, coaches and officials (many of whom I consider my friends), who continue to grant me such a unique and wonderful privilege.

It's a good thing that tree fell over.

# A NOTE FROM THE AUTHOR

Thank you for reading a copy of my book 'Stumped. One cricket umpire, two countries.'

It really is very humbling to think that someone would invest the time to read anything that I have written and I am very grateful.

I have had a wonderful time umpiring cricket in both England and Australia, while strapping on the pads to play again with Shipbourne C.C. was a delight.

I hope you enjoyed my book and that it managed to put a smile on your face once or twice.

If it did, perhaps you would be kind enough to draft a short review and post it on the web site where you bought it?

Just a few words would be great.

It all helps.

Many thanks
Richard Harrison

# ABOUT THE AUTHOR

Richard Harrison is an Australian author who lives in Hastings on Victoria's Mornington Peninsula.

He lived in England for ten years and after moving from London to Sevenoaks in Kent, he launched a cricket umpiring career, while playing a handful of 'Sunday Friendlies' with a local village team, after a twenty year absence from the game.

He returned to Australia in 2011 and has continued to umpire some of the best female cricketers in the world, in Victoria's Premier Cricket competition.

Other books by Richard Harrison include 'The Export Gardener' and 'First Tuesday.'

His web site is www.richardharrison.com.au and he can be found on Facebook and Instagram as Richard Harrison Books.